HER DEEDS
Sing Her Praises

NCJ℥ ℠

National Council of Jewish Women
Pittsburgh Section

This book is a gift from National Council of Jewish Women Pittsburgh Section. Underwritten by the Richard E. Rauh Oral History Fund.

Her Deeds Sing Her Praises: Profiles of Pittsburgh Jewish Women

Copyright © 2016 by Eileen Lane, Eric Lidji, Lois Michaels

All rights reserved. No part of this book/manuscript may be reproduced in any form or by any electronic or mechanical means, including information or storage and retrieval systems, without permission in writing from the author and the National Council of Jewish Women, Pittsburgh Section.

Printed in the United States of America.

ISBN: 978-1-63385-155-9

Library of Congress Control Number: 2016910734

Designed by
Melissa Neely

Published by
Word Association Publishers
205 Fifth Avenue
Tarentum, Pennsylvania 15084

www.wordassociation.com
1.800.827.7903

Foreword

T he idea for this book grew out of several years of conversations between the two of us. We had enjoyed working
together on other projects, and although we are of different
generations, we found we shared a love of history and a "can
do" attitude. We had both spent years in communal service,
particularly with organizations dedicated to women's interests
and issues. We also discovered a mutual admiration for women
who had come before us, women who had accomplished
much despite considerable personal and cultural obstacles.
Some of these women we had known personally, others only
by reputation. The determination to produce a written legacy
of some of these notable Jewish women came from our desire
to share their inspirational stories with others.

We convened an advisory group of historians, archivists,
writers, communal leaders and found that their enthusiasm
and commitment to the project matched our own. Soon, we
had developed a long list of women to include in a book, much
longer than we had the resources to pursue comprehensively.
We decided to take a more personal approach, allowing our
volunteer writers to select the subjects they wished to profile
in their own writing style, so long as they could ground their
research and writing in reliable source material. Some of our
writers had been researching their subjects for many years.
Others knew their subjects, and yet still took time to conduct
objective research. Since we decided to focus on women who
were no longer living, we also began a secondary project to
record oral histories with contemporary women. This will
ensure that the lives and achievements of present day Jewish
women can be preserved through their own words and voices.

This book recounts the deeds and sings the praises of 21 Jewish women. They lived in different eras, came from different backgrounds and followed different paths. They were community leaders and social reformers; innovators, entrepreneurs and trailblazers; doctors, jurists and teachers; artists and writers; humanitarians, scholars and philanthropists. Some lived in this region their entire lives. Others moved here. One spent her formative years here, before undertaking her work in other cities. Despite their connections to Western Pennsylvania and its Jewish community, their accomplishments often reached beyond their immediate community and region. Their biographies offer insight into the often-unheralded role of women in American social, political, educational and economic development, as explained in an introduction that sets a scholarly framework for understanding the writing of the history of Jewish women in 20th century America.

The lives of these women span nearly 150 years. Over that period their stories speak to the impact of historical events and a changing social and economic environment. The oldest of the women were born in 1865, as the Civil War was nearing its end and Pittsburgh was becoming a major industrial center. A Jewish population of fewer than 1,000 lived in a growing city of approximately 70,000. Recognizing that government aid was rare at the time, these Victorian-era women used their Jewish values to create institutions and programs that would eventually benefit people beyond the Jewish community. They sidestepped the limitations imposed on them as women by developing careers as volunteers and early professionals. By the time the youngest of our subjects was born, World War II was over. Pittsburgh was nearing its industrial peak and would soon enter several decades of transition into a metropolitan area where education, medicine and high technology would drive the economy. The city's population grew to over 670,000 and its Jewish population would come close to 55,000. Over the course of time, we chronicle women who were able to pursue full time employment, marry and raise a family without being considered out of the ordinary. Our subjects experienced wars, and many the privations of economic depression. They include advocates for women's suffrage and later those who ran for political office, many overcoming the barriers of gender inequality. They demonstrated the value of education for themselves and espoused all manner of educational opportunities for others. Some campaigned for civil rights, others for reproductive rights. As Jews many knew discrimination first-hand. Others devoted time and resources to supporting the new State of Israel. This is a record of women whose lives and deeds deserve telling for all they contributed to our city and to enriching the fabric of our society.

Considerable thanks are due to many individuals and organizations. We found a welcome home and significant financial underwriting from the Pittsburgh Section of the National Council of Jewish Women and its Richard E. Rauh Oral History Fund. This partnership is particularly fitting, given the NCJW's longstanding support for recording the history of Western Pennsylvania. Its groundbreaking Oral History Project provided an excellent source of information to our writers by presenting the actual voices of many of our subjects. We are also fortunate to live in a city with many dedicated and knowledgeable archivists. We found help and support from the Rauh Jewish Archives at the Senator John Heinz History Center, the Archives Services Center at the University of Pittsburgh, the archives at Rodef Shalom Congregation and Point Park University and Carnegie Mellon University Library's Pittsburgh Jewish Newspaper Project.

We extend special thanks to each of our volunteer writers, to Dr. Rachel Kranson, of the Religious Studies Department at the University of Pittsburgh and to our associate editor Eric Lidji for their invaluable contributions. Dr. Kranson's recommendation to reproduce photographs and documentary source material about each woman profiled in this book will broaden its educational value and bring its stories to life. Eric Lidji's research, writing and editing skills are apparent throughout this book. With good humor and sincerity he consistently provided the perspective needed to move us forward.

A word about the title of this book: the phrase "Her Deeds Sing Her Praises" comes from Chapter 31 of Proverbs, which is better known as *Eshet Chayel,* or "Woman of Valor." This poem of praise is traditionally recited at a Sabbath meal to celebrate the nobility of the Jewish woman. In the spirit of its title, we offer these profiles as a means to connect to and memorialize these extraordinary Jewish women.

For what is useful, informative and readable, we thank those who helped produce "Her Deeds Sing Her Praises." For errors, inconsistencies or other deficiencies, we take full responsibility. This is a beginning. Our hope is that among our readers there will be some who will start their own journey to explore and record the history of Jewish women.

Eileen Lane and Lois Michaels
Pittsburgh, PA
June 2016

The Study of Jewish Women: A Brief History

by Dr. Rachel Kranson
University of Pittsburgh

Not too many years ago, the publication of a documentary sourcebook on the Jewish women of Pittsburgh would have been unthinkable. This was not because of a malevolent conspiracy of people who wanted to systematically silence women's voices, but rather because of widely accepted assumptions about what constituted the stuff of history.

When history emerged as a professional field in the 19th century, practitioners recorded tales of diplomacy, of great kings and leaders, and of military battles won and lost. They presented these subjects as the "universal" history of humankind, without considering that there might be much more to world history than the record of national conflict. They also did not recognize that nearly all of the personalities who made it into their narratives were male, wealthy, Christian, and of European descent, or that the pasts of people who did not match that profile might also be worth preserving, analyzing, and recounting.

Slowly, beginning in the early 20th century, certain scholars began to point out that what most historians presented as a "universal" history was, in actuality, a very particular narrative focusing on the nationalist aspirations of elite white men. Scholars like Charles and Mary Beard began to write about the history of the poor, while W.E.B. Du Bois began to consider African Americans as scholarly subjects. And by 1933, Mary Ritter Beard published *America through Women's Eyes*, the first contemporary work of history that placed women at the center of the story. It was not until the feminist movement of the 1970s, however, that women's pasts became a common focus of historical inquiry both in the academy and more popular venues.

The field of Jewish history developed alongside the professional field of history, but rarely intersected with it. Needless to say, the diplomatic and military histories taught by 19th century historians rarely included Jews, a people who possessed neither country nor army. Still, under the radar of mainstream historians, Jewish intellectuals were quietly composing histories of the Jewish people. The early 19th century saw the development of the *Wissenschaft des Judentums,* a movement aimed at bringing modern academic tools of inquiry to the study of Jewish culture. Though the men of the *Wissenschaft* (and they were all men) were never embraced by major universities of the time, they still produced some remarkable works of scholarship. By 1853, Heinrich Graetz, a follower of this movement, published the first volume of his magisterial, four-volume *Geschichte der Juden (History of the Jews).* Working through the same gendered lens as the leading historians of his day, Graetz presented the particular history of Jewish men as the universal story of the Jewish people.

The social movements of the late 1960s and 1970s transformed the field of Jewish history much as it transformed the study of women's history. While a handful of Jewish Studies professors were hired by major universities in the early 20th century, it was not until the 1970s, when the study of minorities became acceptable in the academy, that universities began to develop Jewish studies programs and departments. Soon, scholars combined the fast-growing fields of Jewish history and women's history. By 1976, Paula Hyman, Charlotte Baum, and Sonya Michel published *The Jewish Woman in America*, the first of what became many volumes of Jewish women's history.

The relatively new field of Jewish women's history faced unprecedented challenges. A main obstacle was one of sources. Since the lives of women were not always recognized as being historically significant, too many Jewish women did not save the primary sources that would enable later historians to document their lives. This impediment becomes particularly daunting when trying to write the histories of "everyday" women who achieved neither fame nor fortune, but whose lives are nonetheless significant to the overall project of Jewish and world history.

Still, practitioners of Jewish women's history have persevered in spite of the difficulties. They have produced a wealth of academic and popular volumes that placed women at the center of Jewish history, and developed public history projects, such as the Jewish Women's Archive, that have brought the history of Jewish women to the public in new and innovative ways. In the process, these historians have transformed the study of Jewish history. They have proved that we cannot understand the richness of the Jewish experience without examining the stories of Jewish women. And, in more recent years, they have shown us how illuminating it can be to analyze the impact of gender not only on the lives of Jewish women, but also on the lives of Jewish men.

I am very pleased that this volume will add to the rich and varied corpus of Jewish women's history by highlighting some of the Jewish women who lived, loved, and worked in the Pittsburgh region. This volume recounts the fascinating history—much of it largely unknown—of individuals who navigated the city of Pittsburgh as women and as Jews. Both in spite of, and because of, their status as Jewish women, they found ways to contribute to their home city and beyond.

With this volume, editors Eileen Lane and Lois Michaels have created both a model and a resource for future historians. Enthusiasts of local history would be well advised to use some of their techniques to uncover the forgotten histories of Jewish women in their own communities. Furthermore, by including primary sources that illuminate the lives of the women they profile, this volume also delivers an invaluable gift to future generations of historians who may decide to write their own narratives incorporating the experiences of the Jewish women of Pittsburgh. I look forward to seeing the innovative ways in which future scholars decide to use this volume; after all, the most exciting thing a work of history can accomplish is to inspire others to build upon it in ways we could not have anticipated.

Maxine Goldmark Aaron
(May 14, 1903–February 4, 1996)

by Frances Aaron Hess

G iven the central involvement of the Aaron family in the
Pittsburgh Jewish community for more than a century,
many might be surprised to learn that, as a child, Maxine
Goldmark Aaron had no formal religious training. Her parents
were part of the large unaffiliated Jewish community in New
York City. Her father, Emil Goldmark, the son and grandson
of cantors in the Austro-Hungarian Empire, was an avowed
agnostic. Yet he identified with the Jewish community and was
chairman of the Legal Committee of the New York Federation
of Jewish Philanthropies for many years. The first time Maxine

(photograph courtesy of Aaron Family Papers, 1848-1978, MSS #248, Rauh Jewish
Archives, Thomas and Katherine Detre Library and Archives, Senator John Heinz
History Center)

Aaron attended formal Jewish worship was during her college years at Vassar, when she went to a temple in Poughkeepsie to hear her sister speak on the child labor amendment. From her parents, Maxine Aaron inherited a strong sense of the importance of community service and the centrality of ethical and moral values. At Vassar she developed an acute sense of community responsibility—that one had an obligation to one's own community and was responsible for the kind of world in which one lived.

Her active participation in Jewish religious and institutional life occurred after she married Marcus Lester Aaron in 1926. The Aaron family had immigrated to the Pittsburgh area in 1861, from Germany, and became business and communal leaders, particularly through their association with Rodef Shalom Congregation. Lester Aaron was a long-time president of the congregation and a scholarly and religious temple-goer his entire life. The Aaron family's deep involvement in the congregation and Rodef Shalom Rabbi Dr. Samuel Goldenson's great emphasis on the universal and moral aspects of Judaism were the key elements affecting Maxine Aaron's Jewish development.

Though her great contribution to Pittsburgh was in the field of public education, Maxine Aaron was herself educated at a New York private school—Horace Mann School for Girls, the demonstration school for the Teachers College at Columbia University. Her mother, Maxine Heller Goldmark, had been a teacher. But Maxine Aaron, as part of an early generation of feminist assertiveness to pursue new careers, vehemently rejected that possibility. A 1924 Economics and History major at Vassar, she worked as a statistician for a consulting engineer until she moved to Pittsburgh in 1926.

Her focus on public education began when she married into a family that had always attended the Pittsburgh Public Schools. When Maxine Aaron arrived in Pittsburgh, her father-in-law, Marcus Aaron, was president of the Pittsburgh Board of Education. He had been appointed to the original centralized board at its inception in 1911, served as its president from 1922 to 1942 and remained a member until 1947. In a 1975 oral history with the National Council of Jewish Women, Pittsburgh Section, Maxine Aaron freely acknowledged the strong influence her father-in-law's career had upon her own. From him, she learned that one must be ready to wage battle for what one wanted to accomplish and must fight those battles with allies and not go it alone.

Maxine and Lester Aaron had four children, all of whom graduated from the Pittsburgh Public School system. Her active involvement in public education began with the Parent-Teacher Association as soon as her first child entered grade school. She later served as president of the PTAs of both Wightman elementary school and Allderdice High School and was serving as president of the Pittsburgh Council of the PTA when she was appointed to the Board of Education in December 1948. She also served as legislative chairman of the state PTA for several years while on the school board.

Maxine Aaron served on the appointed Pittsburgh Board of Education for 27 years. She was vice president from 1953 to 1966 and also chairman of the Education Committee. In November 1966, she became the first woman elected to the board presidency, a position she held for three years. It also should be noted that she was the second Jewish president in the school board's 55-year history, after her father-in-law.

Her service on the board was motivated by her faith in the vital role of the public schools and her belief that "the quality of public education pretty much determines the quality of the community." She expressed this sentiment aptly in her 1975 letter to Allegheny County Court of Common Pleas Judge Henry Ellenbogen, requesting non-reappointment to the board: "The quality of life in American cities will depend in large measure on the character and quality of Public Education. It is my earnest hope that the community will continue to support the Public Schools and that the Board will furnish the necessary leadership as trustees for all the children of Pittsburgh." In a 1960 interview with the *Pittsburgh Press*, she said, "The large city public school can give the child a social education he can't get anywhere else, if we provide academic excellence equal to that of any private school. And in Pittsburgh, we do just that." She championed excellence in teachers and quality in the curriculum. In December 1966, when the *Pittsburgh Post-Gazette* cited her as one of ten outstanding women in Pittsburgh, she articulated her position on the primary function of the public schools: "Children today do not quit... They must be educated—the slow ones as well as the bright ones, and we must know how to reach them all. More and more responsibility is being placed upon the schools. Society expects us to handle all kinds of problems—that of discrimination, for instance—and it is education that is the best channel for taking care of these challenges."

During her 27-year tenure, the board became her main focus and interest, to the exclusion of others. As she stated in her oral history, "I have developed a one-track mind." When she was first named to the Board, she visited every school in the system.

Maxine Aaron (front row, third from left) with members of the Pittsburgh Board of Education in June 1966, after she became president of the organization. Aaron was the first female president of the Board of Education. Her tenure from 1966 to 1969 was a period of strikes and social upheaval. (photograph courtesy of Aaron Family Papers, 1848-1978, MSS #248, Rauh Jewish Archives, Thomas and Katherine Detre Library and Archives, Senator John Heinz History Center)

Her three years as school board president, 1966 to 1969, were a period of tremendous turmoil in American life in general and in education in particular. She faced issues including: the unionization of teachers and a 1968 strike that brought picketers to her home on Inverness Avenue in Squirrel Hill, racial integration of the schools, vociferous demands for increased community participation in School Board matters and attempts to get more adequate financing from the state. She acknowledged that several times she felt beyond her depth, but she always kept the board focused on what she believed was its main task—providing quality education for all 70,000 children in the Pittsburgh Public Schools. With superb

Maxine Aaron wrote this letter to the teachers in the Pittsburgh Public Schools system on January 25, 1968, as they were contemplating unionization. The teachers struck later in year. (documents courtesy of Aaron Family Papers, 1848-1978, MSS #248, Rauh Jewish Archives, Thomas and Katherine Detre Library and Archives, Senator John Heinz History Center)

Tell this to the teachers in Monessen, Scranton, Philly & [?]

THE BOARD OF PUBLIC EDUCATION
PITTSBURGH, PA. 15213

ADMINISTRATION BUILDING
BELLEFIELD AND FORBES AVENUES

January 25, 1968

Dear Pittsburgh Teacher:

The Board of Education has taken note of the increased efforts by one or more teacher organizations to establish a relationship with the Board of Education that would follow the pattern of organized labor. This letter is written, following its approval by the Board of Public Education, to all teachers to state the position of the Board of Education on this subject, and to seek the judgments of teachers in developing a solution.

Since 1964 the faculty and the Board of Education have shared in the formulation of policy through the Professional Advisory Commission. This type of organization is, of course, rejected by those who would follow the collective bargaining tradition, even though the function, design and membership of PAC were created by the officers of all the professional organizations, and ratified by the Board in mutual good faith. Among the many accomplishments of the PAC and its affiliate, the Personnel Planning Committee, the typical teacher has gained $1250 in salary increases in addition to the established annual increments during the past three years. The Board is dedicated to continuing the advancement of teacher welfare and the affirmative response to teacher counsel through the PAC and the PPC in the years ahead. We welcome improvements in the Professional Advisory Commission as strongly as we deplore the adversary relationship and the hostility which are implicit in the attempts to impose industrial unionism in the teaching profession.

The Board of Public Education wishes to make it unmistakably clear that we do not in any way question the importance and the desirability of the union movement in general. We have consistently supported this instrument of society over the years, and believe it to be a constructive element of the American economy. Our position, therefore, relates only to the relevance of labor practices in public education.

Under Pennsylvania law the Board of Education is prohibited from engaging in an exclusive bargaining agreement with any teacher organization. Apart from the law, this Board believes that the practices of industrial and craft unionism are incompatible with the welfare of teachers, and inconsistent with the sound administration of the schools. Our reasons are as follows:

1. Schools are a possession of the people.

   There is no more profound principle in our free society than that which declares the schools to be a possession of the people. Whether elected or appointed, boards of education are the agents of the people in the ultimate formulation and declaration of public policy through education. For boards of education to delegate the formulation of public policy by negotiation is to abdicate their own responsibility.

(over)

-2-

2. **The Pittsburgh Board of Public Education is a legislative governmental body.**

   Like the Congress or the State Legislature, it acts for the people in the formulation of public policy. Within its jurisdiction its resolutions are in fact laws. Any organization of teachers elected by teachers to represent them for bargaining purposes is a private voluntary organization. For such an organization to demand a bargaining agreement with an arm of legislative government is to arrogate to itself equal or pre-eminent authority with the governmental body across the table. It is as though an association of postal employees were to sit in equal authority with the Congress, demanding controls over public policy affecting the postal service. To present demands in a hearing before appropriate legislative committees at any level of government is one thing, and should be responsibly accommodated. To enforce public policy by the strike threat against legally constituted government authority is to attack our entire democratic system.

3. **Withholding of services from children is not comparable with the strike against the stockholder or the owner.**

   The ultimate resource possessed by the employee in the industrial and craft union context is the strike. The power of the bargainers for labor resides in the withholding of services. The strike therefore is against the stockholder or the owner. But in schools there are no dollar profits to be shared. The stockholders and owners are the people and their children. To strike against the schools (or with equal effect, to threaten strikes against the schools) is to strike against children and the people. A higher morality, quite different from economic pressure, becomes the issue: Shall the schools be maintained for children, or shall they be closed by the pickets? There is a serious question as to whether society can long endure the forced closing of schools, faced with the transcending mandate to serve children and teachers.

   Therefore, the issue is one of fairness. The strike, notwithstanding its illegality, is not a fair or equitable instrument for the enforcement of employee demands in public schools, since it can be tolerated only for a period of time even under the most adamant board of education, without risking immediate damage to children. This would be a perversion of labor's goals, not to mention the goals of teachers and boards of education.

4. **The goals of all partners are identical.**

   The theoreticians of the labor movement make it clear that collective bargaining derives necessarily from the differences in goals between employee and management. In education there are no differences in goals. Teachers, administrators, and boards of education have as their only goal the fulfillment of children through the schools. The adversary relationship is unnatural and inconsistent in education, even though natural and consistent with labor movement philosophy in conventional labor-management relations. By its nature, education is a cooperative process, resting heavily upon the sharing of many complex responsibilities. By injecting the unnatural adversary relationship,

(over)

-3-

neither teacher nor administrator can be wholly effective. Where
teachers should participate actively in policy formulation in
cooperation with administrators and boards, the bargaining procedure would separate them. Agents for the teachers and agents for
the schools would formulate policy, resulting in the dictation of
policy by force as distinct from reason, even though technically
ratified by boards.

Board members in Pittsburgh have considered themselves partners with
teachers in discovering and advancing the best conditions for teaching
and learning. This has been a team process. Under bargaining arrange-
ments the team process would dissolve, removing the essential partners
from communication with each other. Under these conditions the schools
would become the possession of the shop stewards or other negotiators.
The Board would cease to have a significant function.

5. Organizational strife is incompatible with a healthy school.

The constant presence of the membership drive among competing teacher
organizations introduces an element of antagonism in school faculties
that is incompatible with sound school practices. A good school rests
heavily upon the voluntary sharing of responsibilities and professional
services among its staff members. Cooperative planning, information
sharing, and constructive professional counsel, not greatly different
from the spirit implied among medical staff members in hospitals, are
characteristic of good faculties. Yet teachers have reported deep,
emotion-laden schisms within faculties in Pittsburgh for reason of
clashing loyalties between professional organizations. Aggressive
membership recruitment has resulted in open hostilities toward non-
complying teachers to the point of social and professional isolation.
Good teaching cannot prevail under this condition of stress.

However, in spite of our deep feelings on the subject of bargaining, we
hold firmly to the belief than an even better design for the genuine involvement
of teachers in all policy development can be created. Pittsburgh has been
different from other big cities in many ways, as we have been different from
others for four years with the PAC. We believe that with the help of teachers
we can be different and better in this category. We believe that over time a
further developed PAC or a similar instrument in a form agreeable to the
faculty is the better design which can resolve our present stresses and give
genuine voice to the teachers.

We earnestly invite your individual and organizational involvement in
making this successful advisory body even more successful. As our Superintendent
has said many times, we are dedicated to solving professional problems in a
professional manner in an atmosphere of shared responsibility, mutual interest
and dignity.

                                          Sincerely,

                                          Maxine G. Aaron

                                          Mrs. M. L. Aaron
                                          President

Enclosure: PAC Brochure

support from the other school board members, she persevered and stood up to all the threats. As the *Pittsburgh Press* wrote in December 1968, she "stepped into the presidency two years ago and has kept her equilibrium despite the confrontations of a turbulent era in urban public education." The school system made significant strides in integration, began working out relations with the teachers' union and provided the public with more opportunities to participate in board deliberations through a new system of open hearings and an experiment with having parent representatives.

A Minute of Appreciation adopted by the school board in January 1974 summed up Maxine Aaron's accomplishments as follows: "She has been on the prevailing side of issues and she has had her share of setbacks. But when she did not prevail, Mrs. Aaron was always back the next day seeking to find common ground on which to stand in order to insure a positive result coming from the action taken by a majority of the Board. She has never permitted pride or regret over one issue to influence her judgment on another matter." When she retired from the school board nearly two years later, the board reiterated these thoughts and added: "It has been the good fortune of this School District since December 1948 to have had as one of its leaders a woman such as Mrs. Aaron, possessed with the qualities of wisdom, courage and kindness. They have seen her and us through both difficult and happy times." Similar sentiments appear in the letters of appreciation she received upon her retirement from colleagues and admirers — "sensitivity," "wisdom," "devotion," "unselfish and truly dedicated," "genuine concern for the welfare of the schools and of the children in the schools," "commitment to a quality public education for all children," and "courage during critical meetings."

Aaron passed her passion for public education onto her children. Her daughter Frances Aaron Hess became a high school teacher in California and Pittsburgh and was extensively involved as a volunteer in educational, religious and human rights institutions. She spent eight years as a League of Women Voters observer at the Glencoe School Board in Illinois and was also a member of the Glencoe School Board Caucus to select School Board candidates. Another of Aaron's daughters, Elinor Aaron Langer, carried on the family legacy by running for the first elected school board, in 1976. She was president from 1979 to 1981 and served on the board until she and her husband left Pittsburgh for Santa Barbara in 1982. From 1911 to 1982, there were only two years without an Aaron on the Pittsburgh Board of Education.

In her many years of community service, Maxine Goldmark Aaron was a role model not only for her family, but also for the greater Pittsburgh community—an inspiring example of a Jewish woman who enriched the quality of life for all.

[Editors' note: This essay was adapted from a lecture Frances Aaron Hess delivered on April 25, 1993 at a program on Jewish women of Pittsburgh hosted by the Western Pennsylvania Jewish Archives, which is now known as the Rauh Jewish History Program and Archives. Hess was one of the daughters of Maxine Goldmark Aaron.)

SOURCES:

Aaron, Maxine Goldmark, oral history interviews, 1975, *Pittsburgh and Beyond: the Experience of the Jewish Community*, National Council of Jewish Women, Pittsburgh Section, Oral History Collection at the University of Pittsburgh (http://images.library.pitt.edu/cgi-bin/i/image/image-idx?view=entry;cc=ncjw;entryid=x-ais196440.003)

Aaron Family Papers, 1848-1978, MSS #248, Rauh Jewish Archives, Thomas and Katherine Detre Library and Archives, Senator John Heinz History Center

Anne X. Alpern

(December 25, 1903–February 2, 1981)

by Eileen Lane

A nne X. Alpern's distinguished legal and political career was one of firsts. She was the first woman City Solicitor of a major American city. She was the first woman in the Democratic Party elected to a Common Pleas Court in Pennsylvania. She was the first woman to argue a case before the Federal Power Commission. She was the first woman to serve on the Pennsylvania Supreme Court. She was the first woman in the United States to serve as state Attorney General. Known for her sharp mind, her command of the technicalities of the law and her diligent preparation regimen, she displayed both flair and wit in the courtroom, along with a commitment

(photograph courtesy of Anne X. Alpern Papers, Archives Service Center, University of Pittsburgh, Collection: A1S.2002.01)

to public service and a determination to improve the social fabric of her community. Dubbed the "Portia from Pittsburgh," she played on local, state and national stages. Yet, she was also a woman who balanced a successful professional career with a life devoted to home and family.

Anne Alpern was born in Russia in 1903, one of ten children. Her parents, Joseph and Mary Alpern, immigrated to the United States when Anne was an infant and settled in Scenery Hill in Washington County, Pennsylvania. Though the youngest in her class, Anne was a commencement speaker at her high school graduation. She graduated Phi Beta Kappa from the University of Pittsburgh in 1923 with a degree in education. Her father encouraged her to go to law school rather than pursue a career in teaching. Although he became a successful hosiery manufacturer in Pittsburgh, he had a fascination with the law, which he instilled in his daughter by reading her the courtroom speeches of Clarence Darrow rather than fairy tales. She graduated with honors from the University of Pittsburgh School of Law in 1927.

She was a literate, articulate and opinionated student. As a young woman she contributed a column to the local *Y.M. & W.H.A. Weekly* called "It Strikes Me," where she opined on modern mores and culture. One of her early columns challenged the notion that a woman must take her husband's name. "In olden days, the identity of a woman was upon her marriage completely merged in that of her husband," she wrote. "She had practically no rights, she could make no binding contracts, she was treated in the same manner as a child or lunatic. It was not until the Act of 1848 that married women obtained the same contractual rights as men. Today the fiction of husband and wife being one is recognized as fiction, a fairy tail spun by the judges. And hence there is no real reason why a married woman shouldn't continue to use her own name." Anne Alpern retained her maiden name for her entire career. Another anomaly in her name was the middle initial "X," which she appears to have adopted as an undergraduate. Over the years, many wondered what it stood for; Anne would never tell. Its peculiarity served her well in her first political campaign for the Court of Common Pleas, when she used the campaign slogan: "Mark an X for Anne X." When her daughter's elementary school teacher wanted to know what the X stood for, Alpern told her daughter to tell the teacher: "Exhausted!" More to the point, when Justice John Musmanno swore her in to the Pennsylvania Supreme Court, he said he "didn't know what the X stood for, but he was willing to settle for 'Extraordinary.'"

Following law school, Alpern joined the Pittsburgh law firm of Cunningham, Galbraith and Dickson. Unsatisfied with the routine administrative work usually given to new female hires, she asked for a case to litigate and was assigned an appeal on a case the firm had already lost at trial and considered hopeless. The case involved a retailer who had sued an awning manufacturer for defective merchandise. As would become her habit, Alpern spent all night in a law library preparing for the case. She ultimately won by cleverly arguing that the small tear in the awning was as damaging as a run in a woman's stocking. Her ability to quickly grasp complex points of law and cite legal precedents from memory and her impressive work ethic won over both the firm's senior partners and the judges before whom she appeared.

Anne Alpern was appointed an assistant city solicitor in 1932. Her thorough preparation for cases occasionally lasted

In the months after the end of World War II, City Solicitor Anne X. Alpern
challenged the federal bureaucracy that made it difficult for cities to acquire
surplus goods from the military. In this excerpt of a speech she delivered at the
Convention of National Institute of Municipal Law Officers on December 3, 1945,
she displays legal acuity, political sophistication and wit: "Never have so many
wanted so much and got so little." (documents courtesy of Anne X. Alpern Papers,
Archives Service Center, University of Pittsburgh, Collection: AIS.2002.01)

SURPLUS PROPERTY AND CITIES

Address delivered by Anne X. Alpern,
City Solicitor of Pittsburgh, Penn-
sylvania, at Convention of National
Institute of Municipal Law Officers
Washington, D. C., December 3, 1945.

  The Surplus Property Act of 1944 gives cities a
priority second only to that of Federal agencies in the purchase of surplus war materials. Purchasing agents of cities
have been lying awake nights counting, in lieu of sheep, such
sorely needed supplies as snowplows, fire engines, dump trucks,
tires. When they went to purchase them, the password from
Congress opened all doors, but they proved to be revolving
doors. Our purchasing agents are back in their offices now a
little wiser, a little sadder, and a good deal dizzier.

  It has been impossible to find out what is available. Billions of dollars of usable goods are in the Government stockpile. Warehouses, docks and receiving depots, both
here and abroad, are bursting with surplus. What was there,
where they were, when they would be sold, no one knew. There
was no master inventory, there was no master mind. They never
could get an answer--they got many answers--all differnt.

  There was little, if any, advance notice of sales.
As a result, the purchasing agents generally arrived two days
after the sale. If they got there on time, the quantities
were so small that they were not worth the trip. Or so large
that no one city could use them. Never have so many wanted so
much and got so little.

While City Supply Agents were tearing their hair and the cupboards of cities throughout the country remained empty, others were more fortunate. Large blocks of valuable surplus goods were bought up by dealers. A fancy corporate name on the door, a seal, a telephone and "a contact" man in Washington, was all that was needed. These contact men knew where to go, whom to see, how to get it. They rushed through warehouses like hunters accompanied with pointer dogs with the tail pointing directly to the surplus bargains. It was like being equipped with radar. They had no password from Congress but they had the pass-key that opened all doors.

The end of World War I found this country without any surplus disposal agency. There were millions of dollars of surplus goods but no plan for their sale or disposal. The Armistice found the warehouses with 25 million pairs of hobnail shoes, a million saddles, millions of dollars of cars, equipment and supplies.

What happened? Chemical patents were sold for 2 per cent of their value. Seventy-two thousand sheets which our government bought for $1.03 apiece were sold for 20 cents each. Tools costing 54 cents were sold for 3 cents. Fifty-two thousand bails of cotton were allowed to rot in Nitro, W. Virginia. Millions of dollars of property was ruined by exposure to the elements in Atlanta, Georgia, and elsewhere. The waste, inefficiency and corruption was followed by indictments, reports of Congressional Committees, editorial head-shaking. The loss to the public was staggering.

-2-

The problem of surplus goods was consequently anticipated before the end of World War II. With our total economy
directed to winning the war and our vast procurements program,
the pitfalls in the disposing of billions of dollars of surplus
supplies were known dangers, carefully charted and shown in
graphs in three colors. Surpluses began developing before the
end of World War II when certain equipment became obsolete or
had deteriorated. Surplus sales were conducted by the various
war agencies in 1944. There were nine such agencies in possession of surplus.

What happened? One of the first surplus sales
conducted involved the sale of 100,000 dry-cell batteries for
which the government had paid $200,000 of tax money. They
were sold at Ogden for $125.00. No, I did not say $125,000,
but $125! This sale was not the result of corruption but of
inaptitude. But it showed the dangers ahead.

The Mead Committee which began investigating the
disposal of war surpluses from the very beginning, reported the
sale in Detroit of new cutting tools which cost the Government
$1,721,136 for $36,924. The need for an overall policy and
a central administration was obvious.

In an attempt to avert the sorry spectacle that
followed World War I, as a result of an unplanned program for
disposal of surplus war goods, our Congress in 1944 passed the
Surplus Property Act, establishing basic principles for
the handling of this tremendous problem. It was thought that

all night; it is said she came to know the night cleaners at City Hall by name. Within five months, on the strength of her successful handling of many difficult cases, she was promoted to First Assistant Solicitor over 25 other candidates. Her next promotion was suspiciously longer in coming, which may have had more to do with her gender than with her abilities. Her advancement ultimately was the result of politics. After defending newly elected Mayor Cornelius Scully on a trumped up charge of voter irregularities, she was appointed City Solicitor. Challenges persisted, though. Some members of the Jewish community reportedly challenged her subsequent reappointment to the position by Mayor David Lawrence. Having earned a reputation for unimpeachable integrity, she was seen as being less amenable to bribes or favors, as she once explained to her daughter.

As City Solicitor, Alpern championed smoke control, slum clearance, improved public housing, reduced public transportation fares and utility rates, restaurant grading, educational reform and public hospital improvements. Many of her initiatives provided the legal foundation of the city's burgeoning renaissance. She worked to expose and eliminate corruption in several local municipalities and forced a readjustment of tax rates, which corrected inequities that had significantly disadvantaged small taxpayers. She gained recognition and popularity for her efforts to protect consumers, especially in her battles with utility companies and the Public Utility Commission, which, in one of her well-known courtroom witticisms, she called "The Public Futility Commission." She labeled its rate increases "The Overcharge of the Light Brigade." Her beliefs extended beyond party lines. In 1946, she alienated many of her union supporters in the Democratic

Party by obtaining a temporary injunction against striking Duquesne Light employees to avoid blackouts. She carved out a specialization in utility law and regulations. She was the first woman to practice before the State Public Utility Commission and the Federal Power Commission, which led President John F. Kennedy, in one of his first important appointments, to ask her to chair the Federal Power Commission in 1961; she declined, for unknown reasons.

In 1952, Alpern ran for a seat on the Allegheny County Court of Common Pleas and won in a landslide. Believing

Judge Anne X. Alpern (seated, right) with First Lady Eleanor Roosevelt, Judge Samuel Weiss (standing left), Mayor David L. Lawrence (second from left), and Judge Henry Ellenbogen (third from right). Alpern was the first woman to serve on the Pennsylvania Supreme Court. (photograph courtesy of Anne X. Alpern Papers, Archives Service Center, University of Pittsburgh, Collection: A1S.2002.01)

that "justice delayed, was justice denied," she took a special interest in reducing the backlog of cases in Pennsylvania courts. One year, she disposed 1,000 cases in pretrial settlements while the 16 other Common Pleas judges handled 364 cases combined.

In 1959, David L. Lawrence, who was now Governor of Pennsylvania, appointed Alpern to Attorney General. They forged a relationship of mutual trust during her time in his mayoral administration, and he admired her intellect, integrity and ability to get things done. As Attorney General, she enacted regulations to prevent abuse of money donated to public charities, attempted to create a state-level Division of Consumer Protection, worked to regulate milk prices and enforce food sanitation laws and began an investigation into allegations of voting fraud against the Democratic Party in Philadelphia. Among her most highly regarded achievements was opening the Barnes Collection in suburban Philadelphia, said to be the greatest private art collection in the world, to public view in exchange for retention of its tax-exempt status.

In 1961, Governor Lawrence appointed Alpern to fill a vacancy on the State Supreme Court, making her the first female juror in the 240-year history of the court. The distinction was short-lived. Several months later, she narrowly lost her bid for a full-term to Allegheny County Judge Henry X. O'Brien. Writing in the *Pittsburgh Post-Gazette*, Thomas Snyder speculated that Justice Alpern had lost because she had antagonized the Democratic Party machine in Philadelphia by investigating claims of voter fraud and had opposed corporate utility companies as City Solicitor, and because she was a woman. Governor Lawrence appointed Alpern to the seat O'Brien had vacated on the Allegheny Country Court of Commons Pleas. She maintained that seat until her retirement from public office in 1974. She subsequently joined the Pittsburgh law firm of Berkman, Ruslander, Pohl, Lieber and Engel, where she stayed until her death in 1981.

Alpern brought the same verve and energy to her home life as she brought to her professional life. In 1937 she married Irwin Swiss, who was a lawyer in the office of the City Solicitor. He served on the legal staff of the Federal Housing Administration and as an assistant United States Attorney. He was killed by a truck as he crossed an icy street near their home in 1960. They had one child, Marsha, born in 1940, who also became a lawyer. Judge Alpern entertained a wide circle of friends at her Beechwood Boulevard home. She took great interest in interior decoration and gardening and was considered to be a gourmet cook. A self-reported insomniac, she required less than five hours sleep each night and was said to have read at least one non-legal book a day. Her eclectic tastes ranged from best sellers to Proust. She even tried her hand at writing, including a courtroom drama titled, "So Help Me God" and several short stories with legal themes. Always meticulously groomed, she was a regular theatregoer and concertgoer and maintained her childhood hobbies of ice-skating and horseback riding into adulthood.

Anne Alpern was involved in a number of civic and professional associations. She was a member of the Pittsburgh Parking Authority and a board member of Action Housing, the Federation of Jewish Philanthropies and other organizations. As City Solicitor, she became the first—and for a long time the only—woman member of the National Institute of Municipal Law Officers and was its president in 1947-48. She was particularly remembered for a speech she gave at its annual conference in December 1945 when she excoriated the Surplus Property Board for allowing middlemen, rather than cities, to purchase and profit from surplus war material. Although the city had budgeted $2 million for these purchases, it had only spent $148.50. With her usual biting wit, Alpern quipped, "Never before have so many wanted so much and got so little." The recipient of many awards and honors, in 1952 she was named a Distinguished Daughter of Pennsylvania, the first such honor for a Jewish woman from Western Pennsylvania. In 1962 the University of Pittsburgh conferred on her an honorary Doctor of Laws.

Alpern was always cognizant of her Jewish roots. While not particularly observant, she felt a responsibility to advance Jewish causes. She served on the editorial advisory board of *The Jewish Observer*. She sat on the board of the local Federation of Jewish Philanthropies and was the chair and solicitor of the Municipal Workers Division for the local United Jewish Fund. She also committed her considerably influential voice to raising funds for the National Jewish Hospital in Denver. Influenced partly by her husband's affiliations in Zionist circles, she was a fervent supporter of the new Jewish state and delivered many passionate speeches to Jewish organizations, several emphasizing the outstanding work of Jerusalem's Hadassah Hospital.

Alpern was legendary in her time for doing everything well, whether it was arguing before a court or sewing dolls' clothes for her daughter. Her intellect and legal acumen were matched by her championship of the public interest and deep concern for individual rights. At the same time as she broke barriers in her professional career and reached heights of public service few women had before her, she enjoyed a rich and satisfying personal life. "Competency has no sex," she said. "All doors are open to both sexes. The only limitations are ability and industry. I work harder than anyone else." She was a true trailblazer and role model for her contemporaries and for future generations of women. In 1994, the Pennsylvania Bar Association established the Anne X. Alpern Award. It is given annually to "a female jurist who demonstrates excellence in the legal profession and makes a significant professional impact on women in the law."

SOURCES:

Anne X. Alpern Papers, 1918-1974, AIS.2002.01, Archives Service Center, University of Pittsburgh

Pittsburgh Jewish Newspaper Project, Carnegie Mellon University Libraries

Stefan Lorant, *Pittsburgh: The Story of An American City*, Doubleday, 1964

Garraty, John A. and Mark C. Carnes, eds, "Alpern, Anne X." American National Biography, Vol. 1, Oxford University Press 1999

Rubin, Victor, "Portia from Pittsburgh", Collier's October 26, 1946

Fishman, Joel, "Judges of Allegheny County, Fifth Judicial District, Pennsylvania, 1788-1988)" 1988

Obituary, Anne X. Alpern, *Pittsburgh Post-Gazette*, February 3, 1981

Obituary, Anne X. Alpern, *New York Times*, February 4, 1981

Litman, Rosyln, "Anne X. Alpern," Rauh Jewish Archives, 1994

Conversation with Marsha Swiss, October 2015

Annie Jacobs Davis

(April 11, 1865–August 16, 1952)

by Carol Stein Bleier

A nna (Annie) Jacobs Davis, "Mother of Montefiore Hospital" founded Pittsburgh's only Jewish hospital in 1898 for Jewish physicians to practice their profession, and for Jewish patients to heal or die in comfortable and familiar surroundings. At that time, most Jewish physicians and their patients were not welcome at area hospitals. Named for Sir Moses Montefiore, a 19th century Anglo-Jewish financier and philanthropist, the hospital provided medical care to everyone, regardless of race, color or creed.

(photograph courtesy of Montefiore Hospital Photographs, c1885-c1990, MSP #286, Rauh Jewish Archives, Thomas and Katherine Detre Library and Archives, Senator John Heinz History Center)

Born in Vladimir, Russia, on or about April 11, 1865, Annie was the youngest of Sarah and Jacob Jacobs' three children. Jacob served in the Russian Army for eight years and after receiving an honorable discharge due to ill health, he decided to visit a brother in Pittsburgh, Pa. He planned for his family to follow him, but he soon became discontented in Pittsburgh and died en route to reunite with them in England. Meanwhile, Annie, her mother and two siblings, William and Rachel, on their way to the United States and unaware that Jacob was returning, made an arduous trip from Konigsberg, Germany, to Manchester, England, to London and finally to America, to New York. They arrived in New York in 1873 without funds, relatives or any place to go.

A year later, Annie and her family moved to Pittsburgh where Annie's mother found work, making and selling fine skirts. Annie attended the Hancock School on Webster Avenue in the Fifth Ward briefly. Described as bright-eyed and keen-witted, she was mainly self-taught, having had just four years of formal schooling. Education was of utmost interest to her, however, and she made sure all of her children were college-educated. She learned charity, "*tzedakah*," from her mother, who told her "to give first and then investigate," which Annie followed throughout her life. Annie met her future husband, Barnett Davis, "big Barney," at her sister's engagement party. He was a Lithuanian immigrant, and founded a diamond importing firm. Together they had 11 children, nine sons, and two daughters.

A little woman with a big heart, Annie and her husband opened their home for long periods to family, friends, and others who needed shelter. On Passover, they never had a seder that did not include a stranger at their table. They led a religious life and were very involved in the building of Beth Hamedrash Hagodol Synagogue, Pittsburgh's oldest Orthodox Jewish congregation.

Annie and her friends provided food, medical aid, midwifery, and other help to the growing number of Pittsburgh's Jewish refugees fleeing the virulent anti-Semitism escalating throughout Europe, especially in Eastern Europe. As medical needs grew among the new immigrants and space in hospitals became more limited to Jewish patients, Annie, then 33, formed the Hebrew Ladies Hospital Aid Society (HLHAS), with the intent to build a neighborhood Jewish hospital. The first meeting included 17 Jewish Eastern European immigrant women who collected ten cents in dues from each member. Within weeks, the numbers of women in the HLHAS had grown substantially. Annie Davis became the first president, a position she held for 20 years.

In 1905, Annie and other women in the HLHAS enjoined several men to aid with their large hospital project. Together they formed the Montefiore Hospital Association (MHA). Annie became its vice-chairman. The MHA purchased an old mansion for the first Montefiore Hospital in 1906, which after remodeling was opened in June 1908. When the hospital outgrew the needs of its patients and doctors, extensive plans began for a new Montefiore Hospital. Founder Annie Davis helped lay the cornerstone in 1927 for the new hospital. In July 1929, the new Montefiore Hospital, a Georgian Colonial-style building in red brick faced with limestone, was dedicated. Only three of the original 17 women of the HLHAS (now the LHAS) survived to join Annie at the four-day ceremony.

The LHAS, however, continued to grow, reaching several thousand women, and played an active role in the hospital.

As the president and founder of the Hebrew Ladies' Hospital Aid Society, Annie Jacobs Davis was instrumental in raising funds to construct Montefiore Hospital, the first hospital in Pittsburgh where Jewish doctors could practice without prejudice and Jewish patients could receive care in comfortable and familiar surroundings. She is seen here in 1898, holding a cigar box filled with donations to the hospital fund. (photograph courtesy of Montefiore Hospital Photographs, c1885-c1990, MSP #286, Rauh Jewish Archives, Thomas and Katherine Detre Library and Archives, Senator John Heinz History Center)

LHAS volunteers worked as hospital aides, assistant stenographers, assistants in the dietary departments, and the clinics. With money raised at galas and other social events, the LHAS developed a wide variety of projects and programs, which included social services, the nursery, educational programs for children in the hospital, a gift shop, a research laboratory, and new medical equipment for the hospital.

When Annie was 47, Barney Davis died of a sudden heart attack and left her with 10 surviving children to raise. Nevertheless, she continued to be involved with innumerable charitable organizations. She participated in Pittsburgh's oldest Jewish charities such as the Columbian Council School, forerunner of the Irene Kaufmann Settlement, now the Jewish Community Center of Greater Pittsburgh, the Gusky Orphanage, and the Hebrew Relief Fund. She was an early worker for the Zionist Organization of America and Hadassah, and an active worker for women's suffrage. Annie founded the Ladies Auxiliary (later Sisterhood) of the B'nai Israel Congregation, which established B'nai Israel's religious school, and she served as the sisterhood president for 20 years.

In her president's report for the Hebrew Ladies' Hospital Aid Society yearbook for 1914 and 1915, Annie Jacobs Davis described the activities of the organization and explained how its work intertwined with the larger Jewish community. (documents courtesy of Montefiore Hospital Records, 1899-1998, MSS #286, Rauh Jewish Archives, Thomas and Katherine Detre Library and Archives, Senator John Heinz History Center)

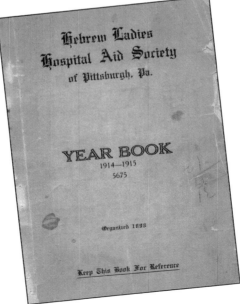

PRESIDENT'S MESSAGE.

Pittsburg, Pa., Jan., 1914.

Ladies·

It affords me great pleasure to greet you on this, the fifteenth annual meeting of the Hebrew Ladies' Hospital Aid Society, to extend to you a hearty welcome and to encourage you with the thought that the present work and future prospects of the society are fully worthy of its traditions and accomplishments.

During the course of the past year the work of the several committees and the members in general has been most loyal and painstaking and the resulting progress all that could be expected. It is my earnest pleasure to state that all our committees are worthy of the highest commendation for their faithful work.

We started the year's work with high ideals and great ambitions, I am glad to tell you that most of them have been fully realized.

The Home Sick Investigating Committee, to my mind, is one of the most important as well as the most philanthropic of all our committees. The chairman and her aides come in direct contact with the poor sick deserving our assistance. Through the able chairmanship of Mrs. Wm. Wolk and her committee the proper assistance has been given without delay and has reached the family in need at the time when it was most deserved.

Through the able handling of her committee, and its work, Mrs. Wolk has relieved me of no inconsiderable amount of labor, and for this and the success which she has achieved, I extend to Mrs. Wolk and her committee my sincere thanks.

The Membership Committee, with Mrs. H. Tapolsky as chairman has been exceptionally successful. Although the increase in membership was not so great as we had expected, it is however gratifying to note that besides the many new members that have come into the organization, a great number of our old members have renewed their former activity and have paid up their dues in full. I trust that this committee will always occupy its present state of importance, as it is the means of encouraging new interest by the new members it brings in and the old members that it awakens.

I cannot lay too much stress upon the importance of the Hospital Visiting Committee, and the good that it can do.

It has always been my hope that this committee would visit weekly not only the wards of the Montefiore Hospital, but also all the other hospitals where there are Jewish house patients.

Whether these patients are sent by us or not need not concern us That they are poor and in need of kindly attention

is all we know, and we have found that the visits of our committees are both enjoyed and greatly appreciated by them.

This committee has been most faithful in visiting the
Tuberculosis Hospital, Marshalsea, St. Francis Hospital, the
Mercy Hospital, West Penn Hospital, and the other city hospitals, besides the Montefiore Hospital, where there were any
Jewish patients found who needed help or encouragement. I
cannot tell you how gratefully the committee was received
wherever they went, and what appreciation was expressed by
these patients for the cheer and comfort they received.

The committee on visiting sick members has been under
the guidance of Mrs. H. I. Alpern, one of our vice presidents.
She has been a very painstaking chairman, and I hope that the
good work that she has inaugurated by this committee's service
will continue in the future. It is fitting that we remember
our members who are ill, and visit them. It inspires a friendly
feeling toward our organization, and engages these same
members for active service when they recover.

The Flower Committee with Mrs. Simon Davis as chairman works hand in hand with the committee on Visiting Sick
Members and the Hospital Visiting Committee.

The various holidays have been the occasions for sending
flowers to the wards of our hospital, where each patient has
had a plant or vase of flowers at his side. We have received
many thanks and blessings for this kind thought and I urge
you to extend the work of this committee for it can do splendid
service not only in our hospital but in many others where our
patients are found. The chairman and her aides also assisted
in Rose Day held by the Congress of Clubs and had the
Children's Hospital in charge.

I do not know if all the ladies fully realize the splendid
work that is being done by our sewing circle. This circle has
just started its work, and you will be able to tell from the report of Mrs. M. A. Goodstone, the able chairman, what good
work has been done in so short a time, and what our good
workers can accomplish if only the will to do it be there.

We are the founders of the Montefiore Hospital, and as
such, it should be our duty and pleasure to visit the hospital
in person, fo note the work that is being done, and the necessity of more active work. The sewing circle meets at the
hospital weekly, and is in position to know the need of linens,
gowns, etc., and is fully prepared to supply these wants. I
hope that more volunteers will present themselves to Mrs.
Goodstone, that the work may be extended. I need only to
urge you to go at once, that you see the pleasure that can be
gained by doing this good work. To Mrs. Goodstone and her
committee and all the ladies who have so willingly volunteered
their services, and donated material, I extend my thanks, and
the thanks of the Society.

During the past year, we have had most interesting pro

grams at our regular monthly meetings. Some of the most
important speakers and lecturers of this city have favored us
with afternoon addresses. I feel that this new feature that has
been added to our society within the past year, is a most important one ,and I hope that the society will continue these
meetings every month for the coming year, as it not only
gives us great pleasure and enjoyment, but it also establishes
a keen interest in current events of the day, and acquaints us
with the new thoughts that fill this wonderful age. Before
going any further, I wish to recount to you some of the
speakers who have been with us; among others we have had
Mrs. Enoch Rauh, president of the Council of Jewish Women;
Mrs. Hugo Rosenberg, past president of the National Council
of Jewish Women; some of our foremost Rabbis in the city:
Rabbi Ashinsky of the Beth Medrash Hagodal; Dr. J. Leonard
Levy, Rabbi of the Rodef Shalom Temple; Rabbi Rudolph I.
Coffee of the Tree of Life Synagogue; Miss Mary Bakewell of
the Woman's Franchise Federation ,and I congratulate our
members upon the interest displayed at this meeting, and their
sympathy with the movement of equal franchise. Dr. Luba
Robin Goldsmith was also with us at one of our meetings, and
her subject interested our members very intensely. Mrs.
Ruslander, vice president of the Council of Jewish Women,
spoke on the Jewish Home. We also had one lecture by one
of the men of the Institute for the Blind, at this meeting.
Twenty-five dollars worth of merchandise made by the blind
was sold. This was considered a very good sale. Miss Sarah
Hilman, the secretary and treasurer for the Women Physicians'
Scholarship Fund, was the speaker at the last meeting. Thus
you can see the important meetings we have had during the
past year.

No less has the refreshments served at the close of the
meetings been the means of encouraging friendly social hours
and has created a more intimate relation among our members.
Therefore I would recommend most highly that this feature of
continued for the coming year. I extend my most sincere
thanks to the ladies and gentlemen, who have so willingly addressed our meetings; also to the ladies who have taken charge
of the meetings.

The Constitution and Year Book Committees report progress, and I extend my thanks to Mrs. J. Klein and Mrs. M.
A. Goodstone, chairmen of these committees, and their aides
for their work.

I wish to bring to the attention of the Finance Committee,
that in the years passed, we not only paid $5,000 to the Monte-
fiore Hospital and $2,000 to the mortgage fund of the hospital,
but also the various sums necessary to pay for our patients
in other institutions, likewise medical and surgical needs of
the patients, also for medicine and nourishment, and we always
had a balance on hand with which to start our work.

Since our affiliation with the Federation, we have had barely enough funds with which to carry on our sick relief work. I would therefore recommend to the Finance Committee that since we have had to ask the Federation for $400 additional, only $300 of which we received to carry on our work that they should not hesitate to put before the Federation for an allowance commensurate with the needs of this society

To Mrs. Henry Jackson, our vice president, I wish to extend my sincere thanks for her activity in taking charge of the meetings during my absence, also to all the officers, I ex- my sincere thanks for their kind co-operation and their thoughtfulness in relieving me of most of the details that I was unable to take charge of.

I would urge a careful attendance to all the meetings of the Federation of Women's Clubs. We have just joined the Federation of Clubs this year, and I feel that the association with this body will enable us to be a power in club life, as well as in philanthropic circles. Of seventy-six clubs belonging to the Federation, I take great pride in telling you, that we are one of the largest in membership.

To the officers, Board of Directors and members of the organization as a whole, I extend my most sincere thanks for their sympathy and kind thoughtfulness to me and my family in our bereavements, and in conclusion, I have only to say that as we are now seeing the fruition of the many years of devoted labor we should take heart for the future, and for the larger work of the ultimate extension of our hospital.

Sincerely yours,

MRS. B. DAVIS.

When B'nai Israel enlarged the synagogue to include a new social hall in 1953, it was designated Mrs. Barnett Davis Hall in memory of Annie Davis. She was also president for seven years of the Jewish Home for Babies and Children. She was involved in nearly 40 charitable organizations and sat on the Boards of most of them.

In 1939 at the age of 74, "Mother Davis," as she was affectionately called, was chosen by the *American Jewish Outlook* as an outstanding community leader for over 50 years and was awarded the 25th "Outlook Floral Salute." Of the 25 prominent Pittsburghers to receive the civic tribute from the newspaper, Annie was one of only six women. When she was 75, Annie wrote a comprehensive memoir for her family, describing her full life with its joys and heartbreaks.

Despite all her community and religious activities she made time for her extensive family. One granddaughter recalls Friday night Shabbat dinners and remembers her grandmother as "loving with a great sense of humor." Annie Davis died at the age of 87 on August 16, 1952. At her death, she was survived by five of her 11 children, 11 grandchildren, and three great-grandchildren, many of whom continue in charitable activities.

Today, Jewish physicians are practicing in all hospitals and the needs of religious-affiliated hospitals have greatly decreased. Montefiore Hospital in 1990 was sold to the University of Pittsburgh. The proceeds from the sale led to the formation of the Jewish Healthcare Foundation, which provides annual grants to those with healthcare needs in Western Pennsylvania, particularly the elderly, underprivileged and indigent. Over half of its annual grants involve the Jewish community. Renamed the Montefiore University

Hospital, the hospital became a part of the University of Pittsburgh Medical Center. The Ladies Hospital Aid Society continues to fund new projects in healthcare, education, and social services throughout the community, and to maintain an independent presence in the hospital.

SOURCES:

Carol Stein Bleier with Lu Donnelly and Samuel P. Granowitz MD, *L'Chaim: To Good Health and Life—A History of Montefiore Hospital of Pittsburgh, Pennsylvania, 1898-1990*

Papers of Annie Jacobs Davis, 1865-c1940, MSS #269, Rauh Jewish Archives, Thomas and Katherine Detre Library and Archives, Senator John Heinz History Center

Records of the Ladies Hospital Aid Society, 1899-1992, MSS# 32, Rauh Jewish Archives, Thomas and Katherine Detre Library and Archives, Senator John Heinz History Center

Conversation with Maxine Horn, granddaughter of Annie Jacobs Davis

Katharine Sonneborn Falk

(February 13, 1905–August 24, 1983)

by Eileen Lane

K atharine Sonneborn Falk, an active participant in Jewish life, was born in Baltimore into a prominent, Zionist-oriented, German-Jewish family. She married Leon Falk Jr. of Pittsburgh, who was from an equally prominent, community-oriented, German-Jewish family. Inspired by her religiously erudite father, she was dedicated to studying and teaching Jewish history. Later in life she found deep satisfaction as an independent woman devoting herself to the Jewish people and the new Jewish state.

Katharine Sonneborn was the third of four siblings raised in what she described as a "Victorian household." Her mother, Camille Goldschmid of Washington D.C., grew up in a family

(photograph courtesy of Ellen Hirsch)

of Czech origin. Her father, German-born Siegmund Sonneborn, immigrated to the United States in 1889 when he was 17, graduated from Johns Hopkins University and subsequently worked in a family-owned clothing manufacturing business. Later, with his brother Ferdinard, he founded a national oil and chemical company with headquarters in Petrolia, Pa. Katharine Sonneborn Falk recalled her father as being literate and scholarly. He frequently wrote essays and delivered lectures on a humanitarian ideology he had developed based on the Psalms. Although the Sonneborn family belonged to a Reform congregation, they tutored their children in Jewish studies at home. They were also early supporters of Zionism, as indicated by the attendance of three family members at the Fifth Zionist Congress held in Basel, Switzerland in 1901. In 1919, at the age of 20, Katharine's older brother Rudolf Sonneborn served as secretary of a group of prominent American Zionists who worked for several months establishing their institutions in Palestine.

From kindergarten through high school, Katharine Sonneborn attended the Park School, a private progressive co-educational school in Baltimore that her parents had helped found. She graduated from Wellesley College in 1926. Later in her life she received a master's degree in Near Eastern and Jewish Studies from Brandeis University.

"Kitty," as she was nicknamed, met her future husband Leon Falk in the early 1920s while vacationing at the Bedford Springs Hotel. The Falks owned an industrial enterprise in western Pennsylvania centered on the Duquesne Reduction Company, the largest smelting and refining enterprise in the area. Kitty and Leon dated while he was at Yale and she was at Wellesley and married in 1926. They settled in Pittsburgh, built a house on Inverness Avenue in Squirrel Hill and had six children—Leon III (died in infancy), Ellen (1929), Sara (1931), Sigo (1934), David (1937) and Susannah (1944). When the house became too small for the growing family, the Falks moved to the corner of Bennington and Fair Oaks, where they remained through the length of their marriage.

Until the Falks divorced, Kitty managed three homes—their house on Bennington; their summer residence at Falklands, a working farm in Bedford County where she gardened while Leon farmed and raised prize-winning Jersey cattle; and, until the early 1940s, a winter home they had built in Hollywood, Florida. As she noted in her 1978 oral history with the National Council of Jewish Women, Pittsburgh Section, she was also involved in many volunteer activities within the Jewish and broader Pittsburgh community, serving on numerous boards, including the Pittsburgh Symphony and Montefiore Hospital. She and her husband frequently partnered on civic responsibilities. Kitty would sit on boards in Leon's stead and report back to him about the activities and needs of each institution.

A significant turning point in Katharine Falk's life was her involvement in the effort to resettle European Jews in the Dominican Republic during World War II. At the Evian Conference in 1938, President Rafael Trujillo of the Dominican Republic had offered to accept up to 100,000 refugees, making the small Caribbean island nation one of the few countries in the world willing to help European Jews trapped by the rise of Nazism. As a result, the American Jewish Joint Distribution Committee formed the Dominican Republic Settlement Association (DORSA) to bring European Jews to the farming community of Sosúa, on the northern coast of the island. Through his connections with the "Joint" and the federal War

Food Administration, Leon Falk was well positioned to assist the new enterprise. He consulted on farming techniques, provided managerial skills and helped secure visas. Some 400 Jewish immigrants reached the settlement in 1940. With the help of Jewish philanthropies and a federal loan from the United States, they farmed, raised cattle and produced dairy products. When immigration ended in 1943, the Jewish population of the Dominican Republic had peaked at around 700. The Sosúa settlement persisted until the 1980s, by which time much of the Jewish community had left, mostly for America. Between 1939 and 1942, the Falks made several long trips to the Dominican Republic to help establish the settlement. Using the German she had learned in childhood and the German studies she had pursued in college, Kitty was able to interact with settlers. She later described this contact as "an eye-opening experience." Her time in Sosúa prepared her for her future role as a fundraiser for the United Jewish Fund Emergency Appeal after World War II.

While her husband headed the overall Pittsburgh campaign to support the remnant of European Jewry, Kitty chaired its Women's Division. She was a persuasive, dynamic speaker and a successful organizer. She coined the praise "budgeting for generosity" to motivate women not merely to volunteer their time but also to make contributions in their own names by putting aside money from their personal or household funds. She felt strongly that "by a woman's example she educates the heart of her children."

Following her divorce in 1947, Kitty moved to New York and immersed herself in Zionist activities. She joined the Women's Division of the national United Jewish Fund and chaired its National Speakers Bureau. At this time, she was also involved with the Sonneborn Institute, a clandestine project chaired by her brother Rudolf. This group, instigated by future Israeli Prime Minister David Ben-Gurion, organized influential Jews to procure materials and supplies to prepare Israel for the War of Independence.

In summer 1948, in the midst of that war, Kitty made her first trip to Israel. Her experiences put her at the front line, as she personally observed not only the war but also the rescue, resettlement and absorption of Jewish survivors of Nazism. In a diary covering her three-month trip, published in the *Jewish Criterion* of Pittsburgh, she described seeking safety in Tel Aviv bomb shelters, observing the training of new recruits, being strafed by enemy planes, visiting displaced persons camps in Europe and watching the SS Exodus set sail for Palestine from the Port of Marseilles. "Today war stopped being something that happens to the other fellow," she wrote on July 12, 1948, after surviving an enemy attack. During these dangerous but exhilarating times, Falk connected with many Israeli leaders and also with relatives who had previously moved to the country.

Her experiences in Israel deepened her Jewish commitment and identity. She became a sought-after speaker after her return to New York. In the mid-1950s, as a grandmother of four, she enrolled in Brandeis University to get an advanced degree in Jewish Studies. Armed with this degree and the knowledge gained with it, she returned to Pittsburgh for five years to study, write and teach. She lectured to private classes of interested adults and also taught at the College of Jewish Studies, which later became the School of Advanced Jewish Studies.

She continued to make frequent visits to Israel, and in 1964 became one of the first prominent Pittsburghers to make *aliyah* and move permanently to the country. Asked why, she said, "It

Katharine Falk (right) meeting Israeli Minister (and future Prime Minister) Golda Meir in Jerusalem in August 1962. Always active in Zionist organizations, Falk moved to Israel in 1964 and became an important advisor to policy makers and intellectuals. (photograph courtesy of courtesy Ellen Hirsch)

is simple; I am a Jew. And now that we have a state of our own how can any one not be in Israel. This is our chance finally to show what we are and how we can build a Judaic civilization." She bought and renovated an old Arab house, where she lived until she returned to New York in the 1980s due to failing health and turned the house over to her daughter Ellen Hirsch, who had been living in another part of Jerusalem for more than a decade. Soon after Kitty moved into the house, her friend and Mayor of Jerusalem Teddy Kollek said, "Falk had provided an example for restoring and rebuilding life in the ancient city." The house became an informal salon for friends, Israeli leaders and visiting political and communal leaders, journalists and students from around the world. She was a simple but gracious hostess. She may have served only coffee, tea and cookies, but her insightful and articulate conversation engaged visitors, who trusted her analyses of Middle East affairs over those of some officials and diplomats.

In addition to her "social ambassadorship," she added to her extensive library, pursued local philanthropic activities and wrote articles for the *Jewish Chronicle* of Pittsburgh, where she had been a founding trustee. She was a great supporter of the Jerusalem Foundation, the Israel Museum and the Archives of Jerusalem. She co-founded the Jerusalem Experimental High School and a community center for Arab youth in her town of Abu Tor "to keep the neighborhood children busy so they'll stop vandalizing my house and garden."

Living about 100 yards from the Jerusalem border, Kitty again found herself directly in the field of fire during the Six Day War in 1967. "The power lines had been hit and my transistor radio was too many dangerous rooms away, so I sat almost immobile for 2 1/2-3 hours before I got up enough courage to get cotton to put in my ears, a drink of water—even coffee, later—and some raisins to eat," she wrote in a July 5, 1967 letter to the historian Dr. Jacob Rader Marcus. Hers was a full life, and she described the time she spent in Israel as "the most exciting 17 years of my life."

For health reasons and to be closer to her family, Katharine Sonneborn Falk returned to the United States in 1981. She died in 1983, at the age of 78, in San Diego, California, at the home of her daughter Sara Moser. Throughout her adult life, she dedicated herself to helping the Jewish people. Deeply influenced by her family's example of communal service and the dream of Zionism, she was both a keen observer and a committed participant in the realization of that dream.

Living near the Jerusalem border, Katharine Falk was in the middle of a battlefield during the Six Day War in 1967. She wrote about her experiences in this July 5, 1967 letter to historian Jacob Rader Marcus. (documents courtesy of The Jacob Rader Marcus Center of the American Jewish Archives, Cincinnati, Ohio; americanjewisharchives.org)

JUL 27 1967

Jerusalem, 5 July 1967

Dear Dr. Marcus:

Your letter requesting an account of the reactions + experiences during these "fateful days" from me, among other Americans resident in Israel, arrived just a month after the Six Day War for Survival began. As you know, we'd been living under the tension of great uncertainty ever since Egypt's military build-up in Sinai, the precipitous withdrawal of the UN force from Gaza + the closing of the Straits of Tiran which occurred several weeks before. At the beginning of that period, when it seemed that the USA, + other maritime powers might take effective action against the blocking of an international waterway, I was grateful for the patience shown by the Israeli government. As time went on + nothing effective was being done, I, like most others here, became very uneasy + was enormously relieved when Moshe Dayan was appointed Minister of Defense (despite, I must add, what seemed to me to be the short-sighted, politics-as-usual opposition of a few elderly Mapai leaders like Golda Meir, Aranne + a few others.)

On the morning of June 5th, I was out watering my garden when a neighbor told me the shooting had started in Sinai. I finished that job, figuring if it was a short war, I'd save my newly set out plants, + if it was a long one, the little extra water used wouldn't matter. About 10:30 A.M. after a bath (wondering if + when there would be a chance for another,) I started putting up whatever came to hand as suitable black-out material on the study + kitchen windows, being alone + not wanting to leave this to the last minute. As I was working in the kitchen, the first burst of gun-fire occurred shortly after 11 A.M. I sat on the floor for a few minutes, hoping the noise would stop but when it simply got worse, I made a dash across the open patio of my house to the relative safety of the living room. Haga, the civil defense organization, had issued a little booklet eight days before this, instructing householders on how to tape windows, what emergency 1st Aid supplies to have on hand, a bit about food + water, etc. I'd tended to these matters during the week, one after another fortunately. So there was nothing left to do but sit in a corner, away from the windows, with my hands over my ears to ward off the noise of bursting shells (there were four hits on or around my own house, I found out later, so no wonder the noise was so unbearable.) The power lines had been hit + my transistor radio was too many dangerous rooms away, so I sat almost immobile for 2½–3 hrs before I got up enough courage to get cotton to put in my ears, a drink of water — even coffee, later — + some raisins to eat. After about 7 hrs, of this, somewhat after 5 P.M., I went out to see if my ear was unharmed. Had it not been, I would have walked the mile to Rehavia to be with friends, as I could no longer bear being so completely alone. But the car was fine + I was able to take what food I had in the freezer, a very small suitcase with a change of clothes + other necessaries in it + a coat + drive to town from Abu Tor. I couldn't go the direct way as that leads past the railroad station + goes up a long hill fully exposed to fire from the Old City wall. Having to go a back way, I got lost twice + was twice helped on Haga personnel who were patrolling the streets. Tho' by then, it was _____ intermittent shelling all over the city _____ station + goes 9. Having to go a back way, I got lost twice + was by Haga personnel who were patrolling the streets. Tho by then it was quieter on my hill, there was persistent shelling all over the city so the drive was a frightening experience. But I came thru safely + was generously welcomed by Shoshana Israeli, who, with her husband, Avner, + 3 children were my hosts until I returned to my own home on Saturday, June 17th. Shoshana, tho born in Israel, speaks a fluent English + for all those days translated the gist of the radio broadcasts to me. With electricty off for hours at a time, my transistor did yeoman's service for us all. And the broadcasting was constant, as besides the Hebrew, there were periodic reports in Yiddish, French, Spanish, Russian, Roumanian, English + possibly one or two others that I've forgotten — including Arabic.

The Israeli's flat was the center of a constant flow of people + telephone calls. We never stopped feeding people + we never knew how many would need to be bedded down (on the floor) for the night. For some of us, living thru the miracle of those six days was simply doing the daily chores of a household with ears glued to the radio. Once the cease-fire had taken place in Jerusalem, it was a little easier. To go out into the sun by day + with car lights on by night suddenly seemed the great goods they really are. And to know that the Old City was, at long last, once again ours was, + is, the greatest good of all. As one bit of victorious news after another came to us over the air, the word "unbelievable" took its constant place in our vocabularies. It hasn't left it because, Even tho I've been to the Western Wall, to Jericho, Qumran, to the north end of the Dead Sea,

to El Bireh, to Ramallah, to Bethlehem, to Hebron, to Mt. Scopus to the Mt. of Olives + again + again to the Old City, that this should be possible in my life-time is still a miracle + unbelievable.

However, right from the start, there has been no undue feeling of jubilation as we all were always conscious of the human cost of so great a victory. Since Israeli officers lead their men into battle, rather than sending them, it is they — the real flower of our youth — who sustained the greatest proportion of wounded + dead. And its a small population, so almost everyone has been affected by the injury or loss of a relative or friend or acquaintance. This has been evident in everything thats gone on here, from the concert given by the I.P.O. for the benefit of the Soldiers' Welfare Committee on June 17th to which the "who's who" of Jerusalem came, to the sober behavior of the thousands upon thousands who made their pilgrimage to the Western Wall on Shavuot. It's an attitude quite different to the one I knew from my American experience at the end of both World War I and II. The only really happy day — + that not one of triumph — was the day when the populations of what was once two Jerusalems were able to move freely in the now united city. You ask about reactions: During the war, and before + after it, I was overwhelmingly glad that I was here during this time of crisis. Not that I was able to make any contribution of any account, but I don't know how I could have stood the frustration of being under the flag of a government that had to put its own self-interest ahead of support of the moral right of Israel's actions. And before I saw any public stand on the question, I came to the realization that now, as always, the long-term establishment of

And before I saw any public stand on the [...] realization that now, as always, the long-term establishment of our victory is in the hands of world Jewry. If they do not come here to settle, & throw in their lot with the Jews of Israel, in their thousands upon thousands and soon, everything this little Yishuv has won at such cost will be lost. There simply aren't enough Jews here to cover the land & maintain a majority in it. Tho money is needed, the real "tackles" of the present is immigration: not necessarily or even primarily VIPs, but just the ordinary factory worker, carpenter, plumber. It's not an easy country in which to live, as move to make & it's not an easy country in which to live, as I well know. But if this need is not met, it is we Jews ourselves who will set back the hands of the clock to the 1900 years of landless dispersion.

Of course, I could go on & on, but since you asked for about 2 or 3 pages, I think this is it.

Thanking you for your interest, I am

Most Cordially yours

Katharine Sonneborn Falk

---

14 Rehov Aminadav
Jerusalem, Israel.

Brief autobiography: Born Baltimore, Md. 13 Feb. 1905. Married Leon Falk, Jr. & moved to Pittsburgh Pa. in 1926 after graduating with a BA from Wellesley College. Bore six children, 5 of whom are now living, married & so far have given me 13 grandchildren. Divorced in 1947. First trip to Israel in 1948 for ten days early in the War of Liberation. Subsequent trips in 1950, '55 (for 7 months), '57, '60, '63 & came to stay in 1964. Meanwhile, had gotten an MA. from the Dept. of Near Eastern & Judaic Studies at Brandeis U. (1956-59) & subsequently did some informal teaching of Jewish history to teenagers & adults. During the 21 yrs. in Pgh. — & the 5 yrs. preceding the move to Israel — was greatly involved in community activities, including some general ones like Pgh. Symphony. But with the emphases & greatest efforts put into Jewish community work. Leon & I spent the better part of 2 yrs. in the Dominican Republic implementing Trujillo's willingness to take refugees from the Hitler terror (1939-41 & stopped by the US entry into the war.) The Sonneborn family were among the early German-descent Zionist & my older brother, Rudolf, has made an enormous, publicly recognized contribution of effective leadership over the years in behalf of

Zionism + the State of Israel. The Falk family of my father-in-law's generation were anti-Zionist but great care + Jewish community leaders. Circumstances led him into 1st, non-Zionism + finally a very positive pro-Israel stand. I myself was one of the original board members of the natl USA Women's Division; later a co-chairman for 2 yrs. of the 1st Emergency Rescue drive; a chairman of the Pgh. U. J. Federation Wms Div drive, + still later a chairman of the Wms Div. for the sale of Israel Bonds, meanwhile speaking both in my own community + anywhere else that USA saw fit to send me. Ultimately, my love of Judaism, of Jews + of the State of Israel led me to recognize that the only way to fully grasp + implement the great opportunity that had come our way in this generation to once again make our mark on world history as simply unhyphenated Jews was to come to Israel to live. I have no illusions that I can make any particular contribution to the State, but I am convinced that just swelling the numbers of Jews under Israel's flag is itself of value, + it is on this belief that I have acted. Whether any of my children or grandchildren will follow in my footsteps only time will tell; at least my presence here focuses some of their attention on Israel. Three of their four grand- (+ great grand-) parents were American born so they are all quite fully acculturated to the American milieu + their ties with Judaism are not strong as they grew up in the circle of reform Judaism of the 1930 + 1940s.

_____   _____   25 July 1967

All the omissions come to light on rereading the above three weeks later. One of the aftermaths of the Six Day War has been a disturbed time sense in almost everyone. So much happened so fast in such short order that we're all still unable to re-orient ourselves to a more normal tempo. So the three weeks don't seem very long to me. Also, almost everyone is suffering from extreme fatigue which allows little energy for any more than ordinary activities, particularly since that "ordinary" is already rather "extra-ordinary"

As to omissions, I'll not go on with them except for this: 1) My house at 14 Rehov Aminadav in the section called Abu Tor was 50 meters from the border on June 4th, with a panoramic view from its roof of all of Jerusalem, including the Old City + the Jordanian hills surrounding us. Now I'm in the center of united Jerusalem, having been in the middle of the firing from both sides for two days.

2) I know that people always, everywhere, behave remarkably in times of crisis, but I can't let this record leave me without my accolade to the Israelis, from top to bottom of any scale you want to set, for taking their place honorably among them. And my personal gratitude for the extra measure of concern for my welfare shown me even by mere acquaintances who hardly knew more about me than that I was a new-comer + lived on the border.

K.S.F.

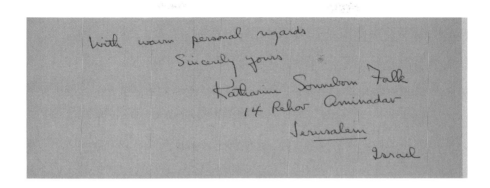

She was a born teacher and a perpetual student. Intelligent, gracious, unafraid to speak her mind, she lived with increasing confidence as a woman determined to be independent and make her own way.

SOURCES:

Falk Family Papers, 1900-1996, MSS#546, Rauh Jewish Archives, Thomas and Katherine Detre Library and Archives, Senator John Heinz History Center

Sonneborn, Charles Behrend, *Sonneborn: A Celebration of Generations*; Library of Congress #94-66671, 1994

Falk, Katharine, oral history interviews, 1978, *Pittsburgh and Beyond: the Experience of the Jewish Community,* National Council of Jewish Women, Pittsburgh Section, Oral History Collection at the University of Pittsburgh (http://images.library.pitt.edu/cgi-bin/i/image/image-idx?view=entry;cc=ncjw;entryid=x-ais196440.116)

Pittsburgh Jewish Newspaper Project, Carnegie Mellon University Libraries.

Obituary, Katharine Falk, Jerusalem Post, International Edition, Aug. 28-Sept. 3, 1983

Wells, Allen, *Tropical Zion: General Trujillo, FDR and the Jews of Sosua,* Duke University Press, 2009

Ross, Nicholas, *Sosua: A Colony of Hope,* American Jewish History, Vol. 82, 1994, The Johns Hopkins University Press

Interviews with Ellen Falk Hirsch, Sigo Falk and Carol Hoffman, 2015

Dorothy C. Finkelhor

(February 22, 1902–July 19, 1988)

By Lois Michaels

D orothy Cinberg Finkelhor dropped out of high school, earned collegiate degrees while raising a family during the Great Depression and established a successful business college in downtown Pittsburgh. She succeeded through industriousness, resourcefulness and an innate ability to make use of emotions in the hardnosed world of business. As one of her former students put it, "When she walked down the hall, everything lit up."

Dorothy Cinberg was the second of five daughters and two sons born to Jacob and Sarah Wagner Cinberg. Her parents were Russian immigrants who had settled in New York City at the end of the 19th century. It was a less than

(photograph courtesy of Point Park University Archives)

harmonious household. Her stern father was committed to traditional Jewish practice and bumped heads with American culture. There were fewer do's and don'ts from her mother, who provided her seven children with unconditional love. Dorothy showed signs of leadership and resourcefulness from an early age. She would later claim she had "invented dinner theater" as an eleven-year-old girl by recruiting neighborhood children to produce an original play and offering ice cream sodas to anyone who bought a two-cent ticket.

Dorothy often described herself as an "aggressive, hard-working, high school dropout." Poor attendance made her ineligible for a diploma from Washington Irving High School. On her graduation night, she told her mother she felt like a "nobody." Her mother responded, "Nobody is a nobody, everyone is a somebody." The comment was a turning point for the young girl and became the basis of her personal philosophy to "learn, love and live," as she explained in a 1983 oral history. "Dorothy's mother helped her believe in herself and Dorothy went on to help untold others do the same," her husband, Lawrence Herbert Finkelhor, said in a related oral history.

While living at home and working at various jobs, Dorothy met a quiet Columbia University student at a social sponsored by a liberal political group. Herbert Finkelhor was the third of six sons in a Conservative Jewish family from the comfortable East End of Pittsburgh. He was captivated by her zest for life and unquestioned sense of self. After a short courtship, they were married at New York City Hall on July 12, 1922 and later in a religious ceremony on September 3. They both worked, first in New York, then in Philadelphia and finally in Pittsburgh, where they moved in 1927 so that Herb could join his family's retailing business, and they could live with his parents. By 1931, Dorothy had finished high school and earned two business degrees from Duquesne University. Between 1930 and 1935, she had three daughters: Carol, Joanne and Naomi.

Dorothy found opportunity in the hardship of the Great Depression. To make the limited public sector jobs have as great an impact as possible, female teachers whose husbands had work were often let go. Dorothy offered these women secretarial training and room and board in exchange for household help and babysitting. Convinced by her husband that she had the ability to create a unique learning environment, Dorothy started her own school in downtown Pittsburgh. The Business Training College, known as BTC, opened its doors in 1933 in rented space at Fifth Avenue and Market Street. It had no money and eight students.

Dorothy Finkelhor teaching a class at the Business Training College, which is now Point Park University. (photograph courtesy of Point Park University Archives)

BTC'S FOUNDER,

Dorothy C. Finkelhor, Ph. D.

. . . . an inspiration in her life as in her teaching

It is doubtful if any other educator so fully personifies her own philosophy as Dr. Dorothy C. Finkelhor, founder and administrator of Business Training College.

Dr. Finkelhor began her studies for a doctor's degree about the time she founded BTC. Since then she has happily and successfully followed the triple role of business executive, wife and mother of three fine daughters. To Dr. Finkelhor, the ability to type and take shorthand no more represents the whole picture of a successful business career than cooking and sewing tell the whole story of a happy marriage. A wholesome emotional adjustment is essential in the office as well as in the home.

Dr. Finkelhor's success in demonstrating the soundness of her philosophy in the training of thousands of young people has brought her national acclaim. Her doctoral dissertation on the problems of young people in business won the Delta Pi Epsilon Award for 1941 and has been cited as a basic work on the subject. Dr. Finkelhor is listed in "Who's Who in America" and has been the subject of several magazine articles. She is widely sought as a lecturer on young people's problems and is the author of two well received publications, **Occupational Adjustments of the Beginning Office Worker and College Course in Secretarial Duties.** Her latest book **How To Make Your Emotions Work for You**, now in its third printing, was so highly regarded by the late Dale Carnegie that he wrote the preface for it. Dr. Finkelhor is now working on a new book, **'Til Death Do Us Part**, which discusses the problems of successful marriage.

Dr. Finkelhor is a member of the University of Pittsburgh Doctoral Association, Delta Pi Epsilon Honorary Society and Delta Delta Lambda Honorary Society.

What Dale Carnegie Said About Dr. Finkelhor's Book

"HOW TO MAKE YOUR EMOTIONS WORK FOR YOU"

"This book shows us how to solve the most important of all problems . . . how to get the most out of life. It solves this problem by showing us first, how to discover what we, as individuals, want the most . . . and second, how to channel our thoughts and emotions in the direction where we may gain what we want.

"This book ought to be required reading in every high school and college in America. A copy ought to given to every bride and groom immediately after the ceremony."

Every student receives a copy of this important book.

Dorothy Finkelhor founded the Business Training College in 1933, amid the worst years of the Great Depression. The institution eventually grew to become Point Park University. A popular writer and lecturer, Finkelhor published a self-improvement book called *How to Make Your Emotions Work For You,* which attracted the attention of Dale Carnegie, author of "How to Win Friends and Influence People." (document courtesy of Point Park University Archives)

Dorothy was the sole employee. She handled recruitment, administration and even janitorial duties while teaching shorthand, typing and bookkeeping. By 1936, enrollment had increased enough to support a second employee — her husband. The couple complemented each other. Dorothy was outgoing. She built positive relationships with her talented faculty and maintained responsibility for all things academic. Soft-spoken Herbert handled behind-the-scenes administrative duties like marketing and job placement. Together they made the school into a full-time job, which supported them and their three daughters. When local and out-of-town family members needed work, Dorothy and Herbert found positions for them at BTC or at their new acquisitions, including Duff's Business School and the region's first Dale Carnegie franchise.

Recognizing the importance of credentials, Dorothy earned a doctorate in business education from the University of Pittsburgh in 1941 under the tutelage of Dr. D. D. Lessenberry. Findings from her thesis became the foundation of her book *How to Make Your Emotions Work for You*. Its message of self-acceptance and self-understanding became the subject of her classes and lectures. "There is nothing in our lives that does not have the emotional factor as its mainspring. It gives us power, or makes us weak, operates for our benefit or to our detriment, for our happiness or confusion," she wrote in the book.

Her management style blended inventiveness, innovation and compassion. She visited regional high schools to recruit students. Finding no suitable textbook for secretarial studies, she wrote her own. She sponsored a dance for a traveling USO troupe during World War II and arranged for her students to work as field hands in response to a wartime shortage of farm workers, which aided the war effort while also teaching her students self-reliance and helping them earn much-needed tuition money. BTC was the first school in the region to offer certificates for medical and engineering secretaries, to use psychological tests for admission and to teach courses on computer use. She encouraged her faculty to earn advanced degrees by paying for tuition and trade association fees. The inspiration for offering a track in early childhood development came to Dorothy while her daughter was in labor with the Finkelhors' first grandchild.

Dorothy was also amenable to change. Aware of a national move toward two-year colleges, she sought state approval in 1960 to turn her school into Point Park Junior College. (In 2004, it became Point Park University, to reflect its increased graduate school offerings.) She recruited a prestigious board of trustees, who in turn appointed her its first president. By 1966, a strengthened faculty and growing enrollment enabled Point Park to become a four-year college. Dorothy's son-in-law Arthur Blum succeeded her as president. Another son-in-law, William Ferguson, took over Duff's and Dale Carnegie.

After her retirement to Ocean Ridge, Florida, Dorothy became popular on the lecture circuit, where she espoused her "can do" "follow your dream" philosophy. She also continued to write and make friends. This charismatic academician left a lasting impression on faculty, students, family and friends. Very often, they were one and the same.

SOURCES:

Finkelhor, Dorothy C. and Lawrence Herbert, oral history interviews, 1982, *Pittsburgh and Beyond: the Experience of the Jewish Community,* National Council of Jewish Women, Pittsburgh Section, Oral History Collection at the University of Pittsburgh (http://images.library.pitt.edu/cgi-bin/i/image/image-idx?view=entry;cc=ncjw;entryid=x-ais196440.128)

Dorothy Finkelhor oral interview by Albert McClain, October 25, 1983 Point Park Archives

Lawrence Herbert Finkelhor, oral interview by Albert McClain, October 25, 1983

"College Course in Secretarial Duties," Prentice Hall 1950; 25,000 first printing; paperback, 1976, 20,000 copies

Conversation with Carol Finkelhor Ferguson, October 27, 2014

"Point Park College: The First 25 Years, an oral history," by Albert P. McClain, Point Park College, 1985

How to Make Your Emotions Work for You, by Dorothy C. Finkelhor, 1952

Pittsburgh Jewish Newspaper Project, Carnegie Mellon University Libraries.

Lillian Simon Freehof

(August 12, 1906–November 24, 2004)

by Martha L. Berg

L illian Simon Freehof (1906-2004) was born and raised in a suburb of Chicago, where her father was employed as a printer. She attended the University of Chicago and the University of Wisconsin before taking a job as the secretary to Rabbi Solomon B. Freehof of KAM Temple (now KAM Isaiah Israel), the oldest Jewish congregation in Chicago. When Solomon B. Freehof was named Rabbi of Rodef Shalom Congregation in Pittsburgh in 1934, Lillian followed, and the two were married soon afterwards.

(photograph courtesy of Rodef Shalom Congregation Archives)

The Freehofs' Report
ON ISRAEL AND EUROPE

Dr. Solomon B. Freehof and His Wife, Lillian

A Reprint of Their Complete Series of Articles

WRITTEN EXCLUSIVELY FOR THE

Pittsburgh Sun-Telegraph

Before becoming his wife, Lilian Freehof was Rabbi Solomon B. Freehof's secretary. They maintained a close working relationship throughout his rabbinical career, including a trip to Israel and Europe chronicled in the *Pittsburgh Sun-Telegraph.* (document courtesy of Rodef Shalom Congregation Archives)

Despite a certain amount of ambivalence toward the expectations the community had for a rabbi's wife, Lillian overcame her natural shyness to take on this public role, supporting Rabbi Freehof in his positions of pulpit rabbi, prominent scholar of Jewish law, and leader of national and international Reform Jewish organizations. She was his first reader, typist, editor, proofreader, and business manager for many of the books he published about the Bible, theology, popular literature, and Jewish law. At the same time, she developed other roles that arose from her own interests and talents. She completed her bachelor's degree at the University of Pittsburgh, taking courses in psychology, philosophy and English, including a course in short-story writing. Her husband encouraged her to write, and she began with one-act plays suitable for the TemPlayers, the Sisterhood drama group she started at Rodef Shalom.

Moving on to children's literature, she re-wrote Bible stories and legends in language suitable for elementary school readers. Later she published *The Right Way* (1957), an ethics textbook for high-school students that was used widely in religious schools for many years. Her goal for that book was to modernize the Jewish ethical texts to appeal to teenagers, and, near the end of her life, she had the intention to update the book for another generation of students. She wrote more than twenty books for children, including plays, mysteries, and holiday stories. In 1953, Lillian Freehof won the National Jewish Book Award for Children's Literature for *Stories of King David*.

Lillian became interested in Braille because she had a cousin who was blind, and at Rodef Shalom she worked with the Sisterhood to revitalize its work in providing services for the blind, a program that the Sisterhood had begun in the 1920s. Lillian became certified as a Braille transcriber, and, beginning in 1938, she taught that skill in a long succession of transcription classes that were open to the whole community. From the mid-1930s through the 1980s, the Sisterhood Braille program, using only volunteer labor, produced and bound hundreds of Braille and large-print books for blind readers all over the country. Braille transcription was adopted as a project by the National Federation of Temple Sisterhoods (now Women of Reform Judaism), of which Lillian was a national board member. As a fundraising project and also a much-needed service for visually impaired cooks, Lillian co-authored *Little Recipes in Big Type* (with Esther Simon Tyrnauer, 1973).

Lillian's interest in crafts and the decorative arts led her to co-author *Flowers and Festivals of the Jewish Year* (with Lottie C. Bandman, 1964) and *Embroideries and Fabrics for Synagogue and Home: 5000 Years of Ornamental Needlework* (with Bucky King, 1966). An accomplished crocheter herself, Lillian encouraged Rodef Shalom volunteers to produce handcrafted items needed during World War II. Until the end of her life, Lillian remained an active participant in the Sisterhood sewing group, creating decorative items including hand-stitched challah covers and baby items to stock the Sisterhood Gift Corner. She also played the recorder and was a supporter of fine arts and theater organizations in Pittsburgh.

Lillian S. Freehof contributed to the Pittsburgh community in many ways, serving on the boards of the Pittsburgh Playhouse, the United Jewish Federation of Pittsburgh, the Gusky Orphanage, Pittsburgh Child Guidance, and the Jewish Social Service Bureau. Though she contributed to the work of many community organizations, it was her firm policy never to take on the presidency of any of them, so as to let others develop their leadership gifts. Lillian lent a stylish and elegant presence to many social occasions, and she exerted her own quiet kind of leadership in her many activities. She was a good cook with a gift for hospitality and for making others feel welcome.

Lilian Freehof wrote numerous children's books and books for adults on crafts and decorative arts, including *Flowers and Festivals of the Jewish Year,* which she wrote with Lottie C. Bandman in 1964. (document courtesy of Rodef Shalom Congregation Archives)

In an oral history with the National Council of Jewish Women, Pittsburgh Section, Lillian said that being the wife of Rabbi Freehof was the most important thing in her life, and she supported him in the ways then expected of a rabbi's wife. The Freehofs traveled widely, both in connection with his professional activities and on regular vacations to Maine and California. When they toured Europe and Israel together in 1953, the *Pittsburgh Sun-Telegraph* newspaper published their dispatches from various cities, and these were later reproduced in a published booklet. Throughout their life together, Lillian kept large scrapbooks of photographs and news clippings documenting Rabbi Freehof's activities during his long rabbinic career. After her husband died in 1990, Lillian continued to contribute quietly to the community as she was able. She died in 2004 at the age of 98.

SOURCES:

Berg, Martha L., "Sisterhood Braille Committee," *HaKesher* [Rodef Shalom newsletter], March/April, 2011, p. 13.

Freehof, Lillian S., oral history interviews, 1975, *Pittsburgh and Beyond: the Experience of the Jewish Community,* National Council of Jewish Women, Pittsburgh Section, Oral History Collection at the University of Pittsburgh (http://images.library.pitt.edu/cgi-bin/i/image/image-idx?view=entry;cc=ncjw;entryid=x-ais196440.142)

Rifkin, Jo Marks, "Lillian Freehof, author and rebbetzin, dies," *Jewish Chronicle* [Pittsburgh], December 2, 2004, p. 4.

Lillian Adlow Friedberg

(December 18, 1897–January 3, 1978)

by Susan Friedberg Kalson

L illian Adlow Friedberg was born on December 18, 1897 in Boston. The eldest daughter of immigrants who had arrived from Eastern Europe in the decade before her birth, she grew up in a close family and a community of immigrants, particularly from her mother's home of Dauge, Lithuania. She was one of five children, although her youngest sister died from diphtheria as a child, an experience Lillian never forgot. Their father, Nathan Adlow, landed in Boston in 1887 at the age of 15, having escaped conscription into the Tsar's army. He sold umbrellas on the streets of Boston before becoming a peddler and eventually the owner of a furniture store in Roxbury.

(photograph courtesy of Corinne Azen Krause, c1880s-1992, MSP# 113, Rauh Jewish Archives, Thomas and Katherine Detre Library and Archives, Senator John Heinz History Center)

Lillian Adlow Friedberg was the first executive director of the Jewish Community Relations Council in Pittsburgh. A polymath with wide ranging tastes, Friedberg was also a popular lecturer on a range of topics. (document courtesy of Lillian A. Friedberg Papers, 1904-1975, AIS.2000.04, Archives Service Center, University of Pittsburgh)

Please return this

Lillian Adlow Friedberg

Communal Leader—Lecturer

LILLIAN ADLOW FRIEDBERG is a graduate of Radcliffe College, where she received her Bachelor's and Master's degrees in economics and political science. She has been active in communal affairs in Pittsburgh. She was first president of the Radcliffe Club of Western Pennsylvania, and is now president of the Conference of Jewish Women's Organizations, and vice-president of the Pittsburgh Branch, American Association of University Women. She has lectured extensively on subjects of vital current interest. Wherever she has appeared she has been most warmly received.

SUBJECTS

HOW DO CHANGING POLITICAL ECONOMIES AFFECT WOMEN?

THE NEW CHALLENGE TO PARENTS

WINDOWS ON A WOMAN'S WORLD

WHAT WAS WRONG WITH THE PEACE MOVEMENT?

WOMAN'S ROLE IN THE PRESENT CRISIS

WOMEN AND THE WAR

FAITH AND FREEDOM

"MUST BOOKS" OF THE CURRENT SEASON

GREAT PERSONALITIES IN JEWISH HISTORY
(Rashi, Halevi, Spinoza, Maimonides)

ROLE OF WOMEN IN JEWISH HISTORY

JEWISH LIFE THROUGH JEWISH NOVELS

Other subjects of current interest available on request

RECENT ENGAGEMENTS

Quota Club of Johnstown, Pa.

Joint Meeting of Peace Committees of New Castle, Pa.

Women's Clubs of Forest Hills, Pa.

Butler, Pa., Branch, American Association University Women

Pennsylvania College for Women—General Student Assembly

Faculty Branch of A.A.U.W. at Indiana State Teachers' College, Pa.

Council of Jewish Women, New Haven, Conn.

Hadassah Chapters in the Tri-State Area (Pennsylvania, West Virginia, Ohio)

Regional Conferences of Hadassah

Regional Conferences of American Association University Women

Council of Jewish Juniors

Temple Sisterhoods

For terms and dates write to
JEWISH CENTER LECTURE BUREAU
Of the National Jewish Welfare Board
220 Fifth Avenue, New York, N. Y.

1

Comments

"There has been so much enthusiasm about your talk, you were a real inspiration. As Program Chairman, I was gratified to have the year's meeting end on such a high and satisfying level."

Rodef Shalom Sisterhood, Pittsburgh, Pa.

* * * *

"Our gratitude for your Sunday evening lecture increases as the echoes of public praise continue to be heard."

Steubenville Chapter of Junior Hadassah

* * * *

"Mrs. Friedberg's lecture was splendid, and we are still receiving many compliments and fine comments about it."

Quota Club, Johnstown, Pa.

* * * *

"I want to tell you how much we appreciated your lecture. There has been such an abundance of praise that we are hoping to have you again."

Beaver Valley Council of Jewish Women

* * * *

"I am happy to recommend Mrs. Lillian Adlow Friedberg as an admirable speaker. She is well-informed, decisive and interesting."

Bernice Brown Cronkhite, Dean, Radcliffe College, Cambridge, Mass.

* * * *

"I am very glad to recommend to you Mrs. Lillian Adlow Friedberg. She spoke before our student body here last year and did a very good job of it. As a matter of fact, we have her booked for another lecture this spring. She has a charming personality, and speaks with ease and grace. She is well-informed, and holds her audience completely."

Herbert L. Spencer, President, Pennsylvania College for Women,
Pittsburgh, Pa.

* * * *

"She speaks beautifully, with clear thought, extemporaneously, and for panel discussions, in the work of the American Association of University Women we have found her most pleasing to audiences. I would recommend her most highly from the knowledge I have of her speaking."

Mrs. Arnold M. Replogle, President, Pittsburgh Branch, American
Association of University Women and President, National Council
on State Legislation.

Their mother, Bathsheba Bravman Adlow, was a traditional homemaker who made sure that her three surviving daughters had the same educational opportunities as their older brother, even though she herself had never learned to read or write English. All four children attended the competitive public Boston Latin schools, and went on to graduate from Harvard or Radcliffe colleges, where Lillian earned degrees in Government. Her brother Elijah became Chief Justice of the Boston Municipal Courts. Her sister Dorothy, who married composer Nicolas Slonimsky, was art critic for *The Christian Science Monitor* for more than forty years. Her youngest sister Chippe did not pursue a professional career but like her sisters had a lifelong intellectual curiosity and bequeathed a nature preserve from a country home in Connecticut.

Lillian grew up in a home with an emphasis on study and intellect, which was common among Jews from Lithuania. Jewish practice and traditions shaped daily life, even as the children grew up among non-Jewish neighbors. Although her father worked on Shabbat, her mother kept a kosher home. The family belonged to Mishkan Tefila, an early Boston congregation. Jewish education was primarily reserved for boys, but Lillian learned Hebrew through correspondence with her maternal grandfather, Reb Shimon Bravman, a scholar who had stayed in Dauge with several of his daughters. In addition to learning Hebrew, Lillian grew up speaking Yiddish at home and English in school, where she also later studied Latin and Greek. Lillian's childhood was shaped by the combination of a strong family, which hosted a steady stream of newly arriving relatives, an unabashed Jewish identity, and American patriotism, emphasized by her public education and exposure to children from a variety of backgrounds.

January 29, 1948

For the FORECASTER:

Jewish Community Relations Council

Like most social agencies the Jewish Community Relations Council
of Pittsburgh has experienced a process of growth which has carried it
from its one-time "anti-defamation" function to its present positive
action program, which involves it in a dynamic effort to secure legislative sanction for civil rights and educative programs for developing
genuinely democratic citizens. It also has come to the realization
that this job cannot be done by one minority group alone but is, rather,
a challenge to all groups--those suffering disabilities and those cognizant of such injustices--to join forces toward the common end. Together we fight for corrective legislation, and at the same time we
attempt to introduce into our educational system the intercultural
pattern which alone will give to the youn a proper understanding of
the manifold strands of our culture. By this means we attempt to
create self-respect and mutual respect, which are the bases of equality
in our society.

There is no rule of thumb for this evolving process. Pedagogic
techniques are being created at this very time; and additional aids of
the printed word in book, pamphlet, and magazine as well as records,
films, and pictures are needed at every step of the process. Our
agency considers it a prime obligation to keep in the forefront of
this movement and to provide to schools and group work agencies whatever supplementary aids are developed to assist in building a generation of young people who will understand and practice democracy in the
true sense of the word.

Pamphlets, books, and posters are available and films may be
borrowed from our office, 400 Grogan Building.

Mrs. Lillian A. Friedberg

When Lillian Adlow Friedberg became the executive director of the Jewish
Community Relations Council, the organization was almost exclusively dedicated
to combatting prejudice against Jews. She oversaw an expansion of its mission
to include issues of importance to society-at-large and made the organization
an important player in civil rights activities in Pittsburgh. (document courtesy
of Lillian A. Friedberg Papers, 1904-1975, AIS.2000.04, Archives Service Center,
University of Pittsburgh)

Following her high school graduation, Lillian enrolled at Radcliffe College. She was among a handful of immigrants' children and Jews accepted at that time. She thrived in the intellectually bracing environment, and by 1918 had earned both a bachelor's and a master's degree. While at Radcliffe, she was introduced to a Harvard medical student, Emanuel Friedberg, better known as Manny, who had become smitten upon seeing a photograph of her, shown to him by a mutual cousin. Lillian eventually accepted his proposal. They married in 1918 and, after a year in Boston, moved to his home in Pittsburgh so that he could establish a medical practice near his large family and she could keep house for his widowed father. The family moved to Squirrel Hill in the early 1920s. Their first child, Judith, was born in 1921, followed by Simeon in 1925.

While raising her children, Lillian became involved in volunteer work, including Hadassah, where she directed educational activities; the Radcliffe Club; and the resettlement of refugees fleeing Nazi Germany. In 1943, with the support of Pittsburgh businessman and civic leader Edgar Kaufmann, Lillian became the founding Executive Director of the Jewish Community Relations Council of Pittsburgh, a position she held until her retirement in 1965. As the only woman in the country to lead a JCRC, Lillian was paid half the salary of her male counterparts, even as she was fighting for fair labor laws in Pennsylvania and across the nation.

Known for her intellect, compassion and ability to find consensus among divergent groups, she gained both a local and a national reputation as a Jewish communal leader. Among her many professional accomplishments, she advocated for civil liberties, improved interfaith relations, separation of church and state, excellence in public education and the creation of the State of Israel, and she was engaged nationally in the civil rights movement. She was a leading figure in a variety of community groups, including the American Jewish Congress of Pittsburgh, the Jewish Women's Organization of Pittsburgh, the National Council of Jewish Women, Pittsburgh Section, the American Association of University Women, the Pittsburgh Council of Christians and Jews, the NAACP and the Aurora Club, an organization of African American women. She wrote articles, newsletters and editorials related to her professional activities, and hosted a local public television show, "Faith and Freedom," in the mid-1960s. In 1965, she was honored as a Distinguished Daughter of Pennsylvania for her contributions to the region's civic life.

A member of Rodef Shalom Congregation from the 1920s on, Lillian was an engaged and committed Reform Jew who observed Shabbat, taught her grandchildren to bake challah and made gefilte fish by hand following a long day at the office. Even in her retirement she remained active in community organizations, served on boards, and was a frequent public speaker. As a result of her professional and volunteer commitments, she had a broad social circle, counting Bishop John Wright of the Pittsburgh Catholic Diocese and leaders of Pittsburgh's African American community, as well as rabbis of all backgrounds, among her many friends and colleagues. She and Manny, who became a prominent local physician, were married for 54 years, until his death in 1972. Lillian died on January 3, 1978, survived by her daughter, Judith, her son Simeon, daughter-in-law Joan Brest Friedberg, and three grandchildren.

[Editors' note: Susan Friedberg Kalson is a granddaughter of Lillian Adlow Friedberg.]

SOURCES:

Lillian A. Friedberg Papers, 1904-1975, AIS.2000.04, Archives Service Center, University of Pittsburgh

Luba Robin Goldsmith

(January 17, 1879–October 7, 1931)

By Corrine Azen Krause

I n 1902, Luba Robin was the first woman to graduate from the school of medicine at the Western University of Pennsylvania (later the University of Pittsburgh). The board of directors of the medical school had met several times before they acted affirmatively on her application for admission, the first ever received from a woman. Luba Robin's career combined private medical practice, teaching, writing, lecturing, and active participation in educational, social, and public health work.

(photograph courtesy of Pittsburgh Jewish Newspaper Project)

Two years before her death, Dr. Luba Robin Goldsmith published a weekly "Health Chats" column in the *Jewish Criterion* where she dispensed advice on health and wellbeing. These columns from May 3, September 27 and October 9, 1929 discuss health, alcohol and toothaches, respectively. (documents courtesy of Pittsburgh Jewish Newspaper Project)

Twenty-six

Health Chats

FRANCE LOOKS AT THE COCKTAIL
(Copyrighted)

The following letter, signed by "an old fashioned mother", came to us:
"Dear Health Chats:

"My young daughter spent the summer in Europe, mostly in Paris. As you probably know, drinking of alcoholic beverages is the accepted thing there, and she acquired a taste for cocktails, which she claims does not in the least harm her.

"What is the effect of alcoholic drinks on health? It seems to me a very vital question, and just as timely in the United States, in spite of 'prohibition' as it is in Europe without it?

"Thanking you for the helpful information,
                              "Sincerely,

                                             "O. F. M."

In response to the above letter, we might quote an item whcih was published in the Journal of the American Medical Association as a translated statement of some leading medical authorities of France. It is entitled "Condemnation of the Cocktail by the Academy of Medicine" and reads as follows:

"Several eminent members of the Academy of Medicine, who are likewise professors at the Faculte de Medicine de Paris (MM. Guillian, Sergent and Leon Bernard), have recently discussed a subject that had certainly never been previously mentioned by name within the sacred precincts of the academy, namely, the cocktail.

"The subject was brought up to call attention to the dangers of an Anglo-Saxon custom which is spreading more and more in high Parisian society, and which is stealthily introducing alcoholism.

Dr. L. R. Goldsmith

"M. Guillian pointed out that the use of these beverages, rich in alcohol, and many of the ingredients of which, such as whiskey, absinth and angostura, contain obnoxious essences and poisons, is becoming more general, owing to the fact that they are not indulged in solely at the public bars, in club circles and casinos, but also in the homes of the rich, where the mistress of the house, eager to be in the advance guard, feels obliged to serve a cocktail to her guests before they take their seats at the table.

"This has the added advantage, he said, that it give her a pretext for displaying her exquisite crystal ware and her richly nickeled goblets.

"The result is A CHRONIC FORM OF ALCOHOLISM and the worst type, namely, that which develops on an empty stomach, creating a grave irritation of the gastric mucosa, with vascular disturbances which extend to the (blood) circulation of the eye (retina), and produce an almost immediate effect on the liver.

"This form of alcoholism, which was formerly observed only among day laborers and soldiers, owing to their bad habits of indulging in alcoholic beverages soon after rising in the morning and before eating anything, is observed today in many society women and in young persons of both sexes. It leads to digestive disturbances, nervousness, anxiety states, a tendency to lipothymia and to syncope, vertigo, insomnia, neuralgia, polyneuritis, and marked weakness of visual acuity."

This opinion on the habitual use of cocktails coming from the medical authorities of France certainly deserves a great deal of consideration. It is rather curious that they should blame the Anglo-Saxon (implying the American) custom of serving pre-dinner cocktails for spreading the habit of chronic alcoholism among the French, while the writer of the above letter fears the

THE JEWISH CRITERION

same results in her daughter from alcoholic habits acquired in Paris.

The question of the effect of alcohol on health has occupied the minds of scientific investigators for many years. There is still a great difference of opinion among them as to the biological effect alcoholic parents have on the development and life of their offsprings, but there is no doubt that alcohol has a poisonous and deleterious influence on living tissues and acts as a narcotic drug when taken into the system.

While individual tolerance for alcoholic intake varies greatly, depending upon the racial background, personal habits and capacity of the individual, there are always physiological reactions following the use of alcohol which must be considered as scientific facts. While it is true that the Russian will drink "vodka", which would sicken a German, who relishes his steins of beer, and the French will enjoy a bottle of old wine with greater ease than a glass of rye whiskey, which would be easily consumed by the American, there is—with all of them—a point of saturation and tolerance, beyond which everyone will get intoxicated, and in due time, suffer the consequences of alcoholic poisoning.

An occasional cocktail, glass of wine or beer can be taken by the great majority of people with no ill effect, but a continuous and persistent imbibing of alcohol will lead to chronic alcoholic poisoning, physical breakdown, mental instability, and social delinquency.

Physiologically, alcohol effects the heart, circulation and every organ that depends upon the circulation for nourishment and function. But one of the most serious effects is that produced on the brain and nervous system. As it is the case with all narcotic drugs, alcohol tends to influence first the higher faculties of the brain, those of—attention, judgment, and discrimination. There is a weakening of the power of inhibition and, naturally, of self-control.

Even a temporarily intoxicated person will say things, be wreckless in spending his, or someone else's money, and show traits which he (or she) would never exhibit in a normal state of conscious inhibitions. It is enough to look at an intoxicated indivdiual with the unsteady gait, fishy eyes, uncertain speech, and senseless conduct to realize that the effect of alcohol on the nervous and mental systems is most deleterious, even in cases of acute intoxication (temporary drunkenness).

To return to the letter: Apart from the moral and social issues, we would like to call the young daughter's (and son's as well) attention to the fact that alcohol is a narcotic and habit-forming drug, producing acute intoxication when taken in large doses at intervals, or chronic intoxication when taken in small doses habitually; that drinking cocktails may develop an alcoholic habit, lower the physical strength and mental stamina of the individual, and make him sick and unhappy for life.

Luba Robin was born on January 17, 1879, in Uman, Ukraine. She immigrated to the United States with her parents, Nathaniel and Beatrice Robin, when she was fifteen years old. The family settled in Pittsburgh, where Luba graduated from high school and the medical school of Western University of Pennsylvania. She paid her own way through school, working as a bookkeeper, doing entomological work at the Carnegie Museum, and acting as part-time secretary to a local merchant. After graduation, she did postgraduate work at the University of Pennsylvania. She returned to Pittsburgh, where she married Dr. Milton Goldsmith on March 25, 1905.

Health Chats

Dr. Luba Robin Goldsmith

"He who has health has hopes, and he who has hopes has everything," said the Greek philosopher Aristotle many centuries ago.

"Health is wealth," says the modern materialist.

"Oh, give me health," prays every human being.

Now, what is this much desired thing called "health"?

Is it something tangible, material, like a food that can be advertised and sold in packages, to be eaten with sugar and cream; or, can it be scientifically manufactured and dispensed in capsules to be taken so many a day; or is it a garment that can be made to order and worn by the person at will; or is it altogether an imaginary state of mind that can be created by faith and prayer, as some claim?

Health is difficult to define in words, for it is neither of the above mentioned things, and yet depends upon, and is influenced by such factors as food, laboratory preparations, clothes and the mental make up of the individual.

Physiologic a l l y speaking, health is that state of physical and mental equilibrium in the living body, in which all organs are sound, performing their functions perfectly and in complete harmony with one another for the well-being of the organism.

When the organs are normal and well adjusted they work quietly and regularly without making us conscious of their activities.

However, when an organ or tissue suffers from an injury or defect, its work becomes more or less difficult and its relations with other organs unharmonious. We become conscious of certain defficiences, discomforts, such as pain, weakness, irritability, inability to carry on our daily tasks, lack of interest in our surroundings, and other disagreeable manifestations which make us realize that there is "something wrong", and that we have a heart, or kidney or liver that do not behave quite right.

Now, what is to be done? Of course, consult a physician who would study the condition and investigate the source of trouble. There may be some organic or structural defect in one or more organs, or there may be a mere functional disorder, that is that the organ is sound, but does not perform its work properly. The treatment will greatly depend upon the findings, or diagnosis. Just like it would be in the case of a piano, which produces discordant music. There may be defects in the instrument itself, such as faulty strings, keys or sounding board, or the piano merely needs tuning. In either case it requires the attention of an expert, for once the trouble is found, it can be corrected, or at least improved.

While a constant state of well-being or health would be ideal, it is impossible for any human being to maintain it all the time.

There are many natural conditions over which we have no control, such as hereditary tendencies and predispositions to certain diseases, the wear and tear of living tissues during their life cycle, the accidental injuries and disturbances, which play an important part in our daily existence. Many are due to civilization.

But, on the other hand, the same civilization has given us scientific knowledge which enables us not only to cure people of diseases, but prevent and actually eradicate diseases which were the horrors and destruction of former generations.

Medical science gives us a new point of view on health. It teaches us that health is not merely freedom from disease but a condition of well-being in which we can attain the greatest development and derive pleasure from our physical and mental activities.

The individual who feels "so-so", or is "seldom sick and never well", or "enjoying poor health" has to be relegated to the past, when semi-invalidism was considered a mark of gentility.

Now we want to enjoy vigorous (not poor) health and feel alive, ready for any task that is within our powers.

We should make the most of our capacities, but never waste energy to imitate and strive to out-do the other fellow.

Each individual is a law unto himself and should develop his own personality to the highest degree, irrespective of the artificial standards set up by others.

Even those of us who are handicapped by some defect from birth or subsequent affliction can reach a state of compensatory health and happiness by developing the many faculties we possess and taking advantage of the rich opportunities life offers.

How can we help ourselves?—is naturally the next question.

Science has given us many helpful methods. In this column we hope to discuss some of them and shall welcome questions.

Thirty-six

Health Chats

(Copyrighted)

"There was never yet a philosopher that could endure the toothache patiently," said Shakespeare.

Famous artists portrayed in paintings the agonies of toothache by surrounding the head of the sufferer with countless demons, spearing and hammering the top of the head and jaws with vicious-looking tools. Many ancient folk firmly believed that toothache was caused by evil spirits and tried to cure the affliction by written or spoken charms as well as prayers and sacrifices to the deities. On the other hand, teeth have been used as charms against diseases by the "medicine men" of savage tribes and as protection against the "evil eye" by some Europeans. As ornaments, teeth of human beings and wild animals are very popular among Eskimo women, Philippinos and other tribes.

From the earliest times, the teeth have played an important role in religion and human relations. Teeth of ancestors and saints are revered by various religious sects and valued by them as protections against injury and evil. Women of ancient Israel (according to the Talmud) beautified themselves with golden teeth or golden shells placed over the teeth as a mark of fashion. Richly jeweled teeth with inlays of precious stones are among the enviable possessions of some people of the Malay Archipelago and

Dr. L. R. Goldsmith

Central America. While among other tribes, in Africa, the young swain has to file his teeth down to the gums, or even remove all upper front teeth, before he can find a willing bride, for the young ladies claim that men who eat with all their teeth are like horses and they will not have horses for husbands. Some Japanese women mutilate their teeth at marriage so as to look less attractive and keep their husbands from being jealous.

The vogue in coloring teeth is also well known. We are told that Queen Elizabeth started the fashion of black teeth in the English Court, which, of course, was followed by the devoted courtiers. Among certain Hindu tribes red is the fashionable color for painting teeth and snowy-white was an absolute requisite for the teeth of a Roman matron.

Teeth have been valued and considered important from various angles by different peoples on the face of the earth, but only the ancient Israelites seem to have recognized their importance with regard to health. We find that the ancient Hebrew law required a master, who struck out his manservant's tooth to let him go free because the teeth were considered "the instruments of life", and even more necessary to the well-being of an individual than an eye. As in many other hygienic and dietetic instances the Mosaic law seems to have pointed the way toward a scientific truth.

Physiologically, we are finding out, that teeth are not only important for the mastication of food, but that their structure and condition often reveal the state of general health and defects in the diets of individuals; they also may serve as sources of infection for other organs in the body, if they are diseased themselves. Nature always adapts our organs to the particular functions which they are called upon to perform. Among the ancients and present primitive peoples who live on coarse foods, the teeth are much stronger and durable than among the civilized races, who depend for their sustenance upon delicate, softened, and often predigested foods.

In the animal kingdom the law of adaptation can well be demonstrated; a lion, tiger, or any other meat-eating animal needs mostly tearing and cutting teeth, therefore, they possess the long fangs, and scissorlike molars; the elephant and other herbivorous animals, who live on grass, fruits and tender shoots of trees, have big double molars with flat surfaces, to perform the action of a grind-

THE JEWISH CRITERION

ing machine. Human beings, who are omnivorous, eating both meat and vegetables, are provided with a variety of teeth, answering every possible purpose. We cut and tear our food with the front teeth, which are called "incisors", "canines" and "bicuspids", mix it with saliva, and push it back in the mouth with the tongue to be ground up into fine bits by the "molars". A complete adult set consists of 32 teeth, 16 in each jaw. This is known as the permanent set. The temporary, or "milk teeth" of children consist of only twenty teeth, which are present in the infant's mouth at birth, but are covered by the upper surface of the gum. "Teething" is the process of emerging or growing of the teeth through the gums. It is a normal function and should give no, or very little, disturbance to the child, though every ailment from sneezing to meningitis had been blamed by kindly, but uninformed neighbors, on "teething". There are abnormal conditions which may be associated with teething and give a great deal of trouble to the child. For instance, the teeth may grow faster than the overlying tissues are absorbed to make room for them. The pressure of the hard teeth (in an effort to get through) cause tense and swollen gums, irritability and soreness of the baby's mouth, loss of appetite and sleep, and many other disturbances that may follow this abnormality. Lancing of the gums (if advised by a physician) may relieve the condition and restore the baby to a normal state.

With some variations the following periods of childhood are about the usual ones at which teeth emerge through the gums:

At 5 to 7 Months—The two lower front teeth.
From 6 to 8 Months—Two upper front teeth.
From 7 to 9 Months—The two lower front teeth.
At 8 to 10 Months—Two more upper front teeth.
From the Tenth to the Fourteenth Months—The four back (molar) teeth, one on each side of the jaw, emerge.
At About 2 Years—Four more molar teeth, back of the others, come out.
At 2 to 2½ Years—The four "cuspids" ("eye" and "stomach" teeth) come through.

While this process is going on, the permanent teeth are developing underneath the temporary ones, ready to displace them when they are fully developed. Therefore, it is most essential to keep these temporary teeth in good condition and in their place, until nature discards them, by loosening and pushing them out of the gums—to give a healthy habitat for the permanent teeth. Great care is required to keep those milk teeth healthy as they are rather delicate, can be easily injured and their structure depends upon the kind of food the child takes as well as upon the general health of the child and dental attention it receives. Even before the baby is born its teeth may be defective, if the mother does not get the proper kind and amount of lime, vitamins and other minerals in her diet. At any time of life a diet deficient in those substances may quickly affect the teeth. A diet should include not only the necessary foods, but provide them in such form that chewing would be necessary in order to keep the teeth well exercised, supplied with fresh blood and polished smoothly.

Crusts of bread or crusts whole-grained bread, baked potatoes eaten with their jackets on, fresh apples and similar articles which demand chewing (but are not too hard or coarse to injure the enamel or gums), should be included in the diet, if the preservation of the teeth in the young and adults is desired.

(To be continued)

"A Home-Like Atmosphere"

El Tower Apartment Hotel

MUNHALL ROAD off BEACON STREET

Catering to

Dinners - Banquets - Parties - and Socials

Strictly Kosher Service When Desired

For Reservation and Information
CALL Hazel 6800

The Goldsmiths left Pittsburgh for Vienna and Berlin, where they studied for eight months. Luba Goldsmith entered general practice soon after her return to Pittsburgh.

"Dr. Luba," as she was affectionately known, worked on civic and health problems in the community from the earliest days of her career. She was the first chief tenement house inspector in the city and advocated for the purification of city water. From 1915 to 1919, she was medical adviser to women students at the University of Pittsburgh. Goldsmith was the author of a scientific paper, "The Aberhalden Test for Pregnancy."

Goldsmith taught physiology at the University Dental School for four years as an assistant professor; she later taught in the School of Education. She gave courses in medical and social problems at the Margaret Morrison Carnegie College (Carnegie Mellon University).

A popular lecturer on health topics in schools, clubs, and churches, she remained active in public health movements in Pittsburgh and other cities throughout the Northeast. She served as national chair of the United States Public Health Advisory Committee. She chaired the public health committee of the National Council of Jewish Women.

Goldsmith's avocation was the theater. She wrote several plays on health themes, including *Who Cares?* (a copy of which survives at the Brown University Libary), a health fantasy, and *What Next?*, described as "a picture from life." She wrote articles called "The Art of Jewish Living" and "Jewish Legends," and authored a play entitled "East and West."

Luba Goldsmith was a founding member of the Alpha Epsilon Phi sorority chapter at the University of Pittsburgh and was a member of the National Council of Jewish Women, Hadassah, College Club, Civic Club of Allegheny County,

American Association of University Women, Women's International League for Peace and Freedom, American Medical Association, Women's National Medical Society, Allegheny County Medical Society, and Rodef Shalom Congregation.

She died in October 1931 at age fifty-two. She was survived by her husband and two sons, Norman and Albert.

A medical scholarship was established at the University of Pittsburgh as a permanent memorial to her. The money for the scholarship fund was raised by a committee of women who believed that "the influence of this woman, whose life service was so far reaching, will always be alive." Luba Robin Goldsmith achieved in her life the goals to which many contemporary Jewish women aspire—combining family and social service.

[Editor's note: This profile originally appeared in "Jewish Women: A Comprehensive Historical Encyclopedia" and is republished with permission of the author.]

SOURCES:

"Civic and Health Problems Sponsored by Dr. Goldsmith."
Pittsburgh Post-Gazette, February 17, 1931.

"Dr. Luba Goldsmith Dies." *Pittsburgh Press,* October 17, 1931.

"Medical Scholarship Planned as Tribute to Woman Physician."
Pittsburgh Press, January 10, 1932.

"Pitt Jewish Medical Student with Highest Record to Get Fund."
Pittsburgh Sun-Telegraph, May 29, 1932.

"Who's Who in Pittsburgh Jewry." *Jewish Criterion,* September 19, 1927;
WWIAJ (1926, 1928).

Interviews with anonymous women for study, "Ethnicity and Mental Health,"
sponsored by the American Jewish Committee, 1976.

Interview with Esther Morrow, Pittsburgh, January 2, 1997.

Aaronel deRoy Gruber

(July 10, 1918–July 6, 2011)

by Eric Lidji

A aronel deRoy Gruber often poked fun at her studios. The basement of her Beechwood Boulevard home was "like a dungeon." Later, her workspace above a suburban Knights of Columbus hall was a "grandma's attic." Had she been a man, she likely would have left her native Pittsburgh for New York after college. Considering her energy and ambition, she might have ended up making her paintings, sculptures and photographs in a spacious loft in Manhattan or a country estate in France. Instead, she married while still an undergraduate and delayed her artistic career until the last of her three children was old

(photograph courtesy of Aaronel deRoy Gruber Papers and Photographs, Rauh Jewish Archives, Thomas and Katherine Detre Library and Archives, Senator John Heinz History Center)

enough for school. Her studios in Pittsburgh were usually modest, practical, accommodating and imperfect—qualities inherent in their surroundings.

Growing up in Pittsburgh, Aaronel sensed few opportunities. Artists lived in New York or Paris, not Appalachia. "I've never gotten out of Pittsburgh. I always thought I would, and I never wanted to stay," she admitted in an oral history with the National Council of Jewish Women, Pittsburgh Section. Aside from a gig as a camp counselor in the Adirondacks, a summer at the Traphagen School of Fashion in New York, and a retreat at the Ossabow artist colony in the 1980s, her only extended departure from Pittsburgh was a mundane two-year stint in Youngstown, Ohio, where her husband managed a factory during World War II. In time, Aaronel accepted Pittsburgh. After she had made connections in New York, and then across the country and overseas, she saw a benefit to living at the edge of the art world. Big-city art dealers could be uptight, snobby and sexist. "I love the seclusion of not being in New York. I love going to New York and seeing what's going on, but I also like the idea of being removed from it," she said.

Even though marriage and motherhood delayed her career, Aaronel felt that her family was complementary to her professional pursuits, rather than an obstacle to overcome. Her husband Irv Gruber was president of the American Forge & Manufacturing Company in McKees Rocks, which not only provided her financial security (although, as she was quick to note, she earned her keep as an artist), but also more specific perks. He knew where to scrounge for scrap, and he let her use his forge on weekends. His support extended beyond mere accommodation. When she took evening art classes, he would do the dishes. When she needed supplies, he would stretch canvases and frame paintings. When she booked out-of-town exhibits, he would haul her works to faraway cities. Her children all inherited her artistic eye—even a son who chose a more practical profession. When Aaronel would get disgusted with the business end of being an artist, her children would push her to consider new galleries and new opportunities.

Domesticity benefitted her art. Creatively, Aaronel was primarily concerned with beauty, which she expressed firstly through composition. She had learned the pleasures of orderliness as a child. Her father, Joseph Israel DeRoy, a successful dentist, was very neat and attracted to fine things, particularly clothing. Her mother, Bessie Leyser DeRoy, was refined and cultured—a Southern belle who had attended finishing school and was a talented seamstress. In their home on Darlington Road, in Squirrel Hill, a block from the sculpted trails of Schenley Park, everything had a place and was kept in it. "Our house was bright and airy and I think that helped to influence me to like these things," Aaronel said.

When Aaronel and Irv left Squirrel Hill for suburban Churchill, in 1966, they chose a contemporary home by architect Tasso Katselas, rather than one of the brick townhouses or mansions so common throughout the rest of the region. Still, the influence of her childhood could be felt in the art she displayed throughout her home and also in her large garden, which she called "a living painting or a living sculpture." This sensibility also suffused her art. Though she kept pace with the changes occurring internationally in contemporary art, her work aspired to the simple qualities of a floral bouquet or a decorating scheme: to be measured, balanced and neatly composed.

She came to art through the practical concerns of fashion and design. Her first job was selling jewelry at Rosenbaum's Department Store. While studying costume economics at the Carnegie Institute of Technology (now Carnegie Mellon University), she worked as a fashion fabric coordinator for local fashion icon Eleanor Reamer at Kaufmann's Department Store. As a child, accompanying her mother to the Carnegie Institute, Aaronel was uninterested in contemporary art. "In those days, they mostly had nudes lying on couches and things like that... I don't think it inspired me to much more than some giggles," she said.

Little by little, she approached fine art. Allderdice High School placed her in a special art class. Soon, she was studying with the painter and legendary professor Samuel Rosenberg at the Young Men's and Women's Hebrew Association in Oakland. At Carnegie Tech, while studying fashion at the Margaret Morrison Carnegie College for women, she also slipped over to the College of Fine Arts to study painting with Rosenberg, the Munsell color system with Wilfred Readio and design with Robert Lepper, the forward-thinking professor who would later inspire the likes of Andy Warhol, Philip Pearlstein and Mel Bochner.

This was the best artistic pedigree available in Pittsburgh, and yet, for the rest of her life, Aaronel would remain self-conscious about "gaps" in her training, especially once she embarked upon sculpture and photography. This sense of being at a disadvantage to her contemporaries in larger markets fueled her competitive drive, her resourcefulness and her perfectionism.

By the time Aaronel returned to the classroom in the late 1950s to take night courses with Rosenberg at the Y,

Aaronel deRoy Gruber posing with a collection of plexiglass sculptures before
an exhibit at the Bundy Museum Art Gallery in Binghamton, New York in 1968.
(photograph courtesy of Aaronel deRoy Gruber Papers and Photographs, Rauh
Jewish Archives, Thomas and Katherine Detre Library and Archives, Senator John
Heinz History Center)

contemporary art had undergone a major transformation.
Abstract expressionists like Jackson Pollock, Willem de
Kooning and Franz Kline were now the vanguard. Even
Rosenberg had changed, leaving behind his socially conscious city scenes from the Great Depression for luminous
abstracts. What attracted Aaronel to abstraction was its ability to depict beauty directly. She could use color, form and
composition to express something beautiful, rather than to
depict the beauty within an object.

In 1957, she began exhibiting with the Associated Artists
of Pittsburgh, the hub around which the Pittsburgh art

In 1976, the Three Rivers Arts Festival commissioned a major public sculpture from Aaronel deRoy Gruber. Her work *Steelcityscape* was designed for the portico of the City-County Building but later moved to Fort Duquesne Boulevard. Today, the work can be seen in Mellon Park. The sculpture features her signature shape: the rounded square. (photograph by Vernon Gay; photograph courtesy of Aaronel deRoy Gruber Papers and Photographs, Rauh Jewish Archives, Thomas and Katherine Detre Library and Archives, Senator John Heinz History Center)

world turned at the time. Even so, she was already eying larger arenas. She took first prize in a juried show in New York City, which came with a one-person show in 1959. The exhibition led to an association with the Bertha Schaefer Gallery, which was at the forefront of bringing fine arts into modern architecture and home decoration. Soon, through the U.S. Information Administration, and later through her own dogged efforts, Aaronel was exhibiting her work in Italy, Spain, Greece, Romania and Japan, making her the most international of artists working in Pittsburgh. Others from the city certainly became more widely known after leaving, but few who stayed equaled her reach. Her work is in the Smithsonian Institution, the Frederick R. Weisman Foundation of Art and the Kawamura Memorial Museum of Art.

Trained as a painter, Aaronel became known for her work in other forms. Her interest in sculpture started through a friendship with David Smith, who was among the first American sculptors to work with steel. Smith came to Pittsburgh in 1961 to judge the annual Associated Artists exhibition. When he learned Aaronel was married to an "iron monger," as he put it, he encouraged her to try her hand at sculpting. She started visiting scrap yards to collect interesting bits of stainless steel, aluminum and bronze. One of the pieces she found was a rounded square, which became a signature shape, seen most distinctively in *Steelcityscape*, a seventeen-foot monument designed for the portico of the City-County Building in downtown. It is now installed in Mellon Park, along Penn Avenue in the East End. The rounded square perfectly encapsulates the appeal of her art—strength tempered by elegance. Even her stationery from these years had rounded edges.

When escalating costs and logistical concerns made metal impractical, Aaronel turned to acrylics. These are her definitive works. The smoothness and clarity of materials like lucite and plexiglass allowed her to manipulate light, color and form to a far greater degree than she had ever been able to accomplish with paint. Her explorations of the materials were a constant attempt to grab and hold the attention of viewers. She began by vacuum-forming rounded squares, triangles, cubes and domes, which she would assemble into deceptively simple configurations. Over time, she dyed these components in a broad spectrum of transparent colors and incorporated motion through hidden motors. If viewers took the time to walk around her sculptures, or watch them turn, they would find an increasingly intricate range of colors and shapes created by the interplay of individual parts. "I always felt that what I was interested in was to give the viewer a momentary bit of pleasure. Because most of the time people don't stop to look longer than a few minutes, and if you can mesmerize them a little bit longer, like with these pieces that move and turn and so forth, I think when you're going to live with something, it's kind of wonderful to have something that can absorb you a little bit longer," she said.

Her interest in beautiful things might have seemed trivial if not for an undeniable edge running through her work. Although she rejected "ugly art," with its "drips and messes" and its "muddy colors," she understood the impulse behind it. She was certainly familiar with the ugliness of personal tragedy. Her father had died when she was a teenager. Her only sibling, a half-sister, survived infantile paralysis. As an adult, Aaronel lost a severely premature child in infancy. Scattered among her typically bright, clear and calm works are pieces with dim colors, stark contrasts, rough seams and a general sense of unease. One of her most striking and least known works was a monumental outdoor sculpture installed in Mellon Park for a temporary exhibition in 1979. It was an imposing arrangement of gigantic charred industrial gears titled *Holocaust*. A few years later, when asked to define "art," Aaronel explained, "Art is an aesthetic enjoyment which can either be beautiful or ugly." Her art was in some sense a protest against ugliness. After a fire in 1984 greatly damaged her home, and forced her temporarily into an apartment, Aaronel gamely turned to photography, which allowed her to make art away from her studio. Her photographs are notable for their unexpected perspectives and locations. She was among a group of local artists who lovingly documented area steel mills before their destruction.

Holocaust was a rare reference to Judaism in her art. The deRoys, of Amsterdam, were among the first Jewish families to permanently settle in Pittsburgh. They were early members of Rodef Shalom Congregation and early supporters of Jewish institutions such as the J. M. Gusky Home and Orphanage. Bessie deRoy regularly attended religious services, especially after the death of her husband. While Aaronel was a lifelong member of Rodef Shalom and offered her artistic eye whenever Jewish organizations asked for it, she once admitted to be less enthusiastic about giving her time to religious organizations than she was volunteering for arts organizations in the city. (She was once spotted scrubbing the floors at the Pittsburgh Center for the Arts, where she had been named the Artist of the Year in 1981.) What she valued in Judaism was an enduring cultural heritage. She built her prominence upon Jewish businesses, institutions and relationships: Kaufmann's, the Y, Samuel Rosenberg. As a child, she had idolized Queen Esther. And as an adult, the stylish and statuesque Aaronel followed the destiny of that Biblical heroine: becoming a Jewish royal who was accepted and admired by the wider world.

SOURCES:

"Speaking Abstractly," Barnetta Lange Davis, *Jewish Criterion*, March 10, 1961

"Her Newsbreak Makes News," *Jewish Chronicle*, March 27, 1964

"Enjoyable Art," Pete Bishop, *Pittsburgh Press Roto*, May 24, 1981

"Art 'strokes' folks all ways," Tom Hritz, *Pittsburgh Post-Gazette*, June 5, 1981

"Midsummer Musings," Harry S. Schwalb, *Pittsburgh Magazine*, August 1981

Aaronel deRoy Gruber, oral history interviews, 1987, *Pittsburgh and Beyond: the Experience of the Jewish Community,* National Council of Jewish Women, Pittsburgh Section, Oral History Collection at the University of Pittsburgh (http://images.library.pitt.edu/cgi-bin/i/image/image-idx?view=entry;cc=ncjw;entryid=x-ais196440.180)

"Profiles of Success," Jacquie Simpson, *Jewish Chronicle*, November 5, 1987

"An Artist Who Left a Lasting Impression," Donald Miller, *Pittsburgh Post-Gazette*, July 8, 2011

Jane Z. Haskell

(November 24, 1923–May 28, 2013)

by Jane C. Arkus

A single sinuous black line makes its way diagonally across a field of white. It is Jane Haskell's holiday card design for the year 2012: one black line on a white page—a skier in the snow. Spare but eloquent, it is emblematic of Jane and her work.

In her time and ever since, Jane Haskell has been viewed by Pittsburgh critics, curators and fellow artists as one of the region's "masters." Her practice in Pennsylvania—embracing a wide variety of mediums and techniques—spanned six decades, from the time she moved to Pittsburgh with her husband Ed in 1949 until her death at age 89.

(photograph courtesy of Jane Haskell Collection, MSS #1046, Rauh Jewish Archives, Thomas and Katherine Detre Library and Archives, Senator John Heinz History Center)

Jane's first brush with making art took place at her child-hood home in Cedarhurst, Long Island. She was born Shirley Jane Zirinsky, the daughter of jewelry maker Samuel Zirinski and his wife Anne. Both were amateur artists. In an interview conducted in the late 1980s, Jane mused that exposure to the beautiful objects of her father's making had probably sparked her interest in design and her urge to create beautiful things.

She took her first formal art classes at Skidmore College in Saratoga Springs, New York, and immediately after graduation in 1944 became engaged to her high-school sweetheart, Ed Haskell. All too soon after their marriage World War II broke out, sending Ed off to service overseas and leaving Jane with a dilemma: How to pass the anxious days (and make a living) waiting for Ed's return.

Jane seized the chance to hone her skills in graphic design, and landed a job in Manhattan with Helena Rubinstein, *grand dame* of the cosmetics trade—in Jane's words, "an awesome woman." Her first assignment was to design a series of cosmetic cases bearing Egyptian motifs—papyrus, lotus—in the fashion of the period. Liking the work, her supervisor presented the first drafts to Madame. Jane happened to be sitting within ear-shot of the explosion that followed: "Dreadful! Get them out of my sight!" According to Jane, she was "deeply wounded at first" but later saw value in the time spent at Madame's: "It gave me good experience in design, in getting things done, and how to get them done."

Following the war, Jane and Ed moved to Pittsburgh, where Ed's brother "Bud" was manufacturing a mid-market line of office furniture, and had recruited Ed to join him. Jane arrived, pregnant with her second child, but that did not dampen her resolve to spend her life in art.

After making abstract paintings and sculptures early in her career, Jane Haskell became best known for working with untraditional materials, such as this untitled work in neon from 1977. (photograph courtesy of Jane Haskell Collection, MSS #1046, Rauh Jewish Archives, Thomas and Katherine Detre Library and Archives, Senator John Heinz History Center)

Pittsburgh, she discovered, had an unexpectedly lively arts scene, a climate in which she could develop her art while making interesting new friends: artists, art educators, art curators. Prominent among them were "the Rosenberg girls" who studied under Sam Rosenberg, an outstanding artist and brilliant teacher at Carnegie Tech, now Carnegie Mellon University. In 1953 she enrolled in Sam Rosenberg's workshop at the Young Men's and Women's Hebrew Association in Oakland. (Decades later, in 2011, Jane helped conceive the idea for a show at the Jewish Community Center, exploring Sam's influence on the works of significant artists in the Pittsburgh region and elsewhere.)

Despite the daily demands of raising three daughters, Jane completed her master's degree in fine arts at the University of Pittsburgh, and later taught art history at Pitt and Duquesne University. At the same time she produced a substantial number of art works in a variety of mediums.

Her first solo exhibition at the Carnegie Museum of Art in 1964 focused on abstract art. Some of her early sculptures were assemblages made of scraps of metal retrieved from the Haskell Inc. plant. She made imaginative outdoor pieces, one of them a gigantic spider web covered in dewdrops. She was also an early practitioner of "Op Art," geometric patterns that typically give the viewer illusions of movement or warping.

Jane became infatuated with light and its effects on color. Never content to remain working in a certain style or medium, in the late 1970s she began to experiment with innovative materials. Taking inspiration from Rosenberg, who had urged his students to "think of painting as light," and later from the fluorescent works of artist Dan Flavin, she began to incorporate neon, fluorescent lights and fiber optics into her paintings and sculptures. Writing in the magazine *Fanfare,* Pittsburgh artist and critic Harry Schwalb commented on Jane's spacious new studio: "...sufficient for a gal who will tackle Plexiglass, fluorescent and neon tubing, fiber optics, sheet metal, wood, photography, lithography, oils, collage..."

Jane's ambitions were fulfilled when she was chosen to conceive and execute a number of public projects, the first of which remains her best known. In 1985, the Port Authority of Allegheny County commissioned her to design an art installation for the Steel Plaza station of the "T," Pittsburgh's new light-rail subway and trolley system. Named "Rivers of Light," the work features a wall of glass blocks, illuminated by neon — meant to mimic the way lights from Pittsburgh's skyscrapers reflect on its three rivers. The commission drew local and national acclaim and led to other public projects, including a light sculpture for Logan Airport in Boston.

Always productive, Jane became even more so following the death of her husband in 1988. She was a constant presence at art events and a watchdog who made sure that Pittsburgh artists were respected and their work preserved. In 2006 the Pittsburgh Center for the Arts named her "Artist of the Year," the most prestigious honor given to artists of the region. The honor came with a one-woman show, for which Jane created some of her most stunning work to date, turning entire rooms into changing environments through changing colors.

Throughout her career, Jane was part of a sisterhood of artists who supported one another in a mutual effort to gain attention in the masculine world of contemporary art. In the 1960s she shared studio and exhibition space with Lois Kaufman and Elsie Kalstone. But the art climate was such that she felt obliged to obscure her gender by signing some paintings "J. Haskell."

Jane Haskell and her daughter Patti Haskell collaborated on *Spiderweb with Morning Dew* for a Pittsburgh Society of Sculptors exhibition called "Permanence/ Impermanence," at the Pittsburgh Center for the Arts. (photograph courtesy of Jane Haskell Collection, MSS #1046, Rauh Jewish Archives, Thomas and Katherine Detre Library and Archives, Senator John Heinz History Center)

Jane put her full energy into every job she undertook. She sat on the boards of the Carnegie Museum of Art and the Associated Artists of Pittsburgh, the Winchester Thurston School and the Society of Sculptors. She also played active roles on the Public Art Advisory Committee of the Pittsburgh Cultural Trust, with Jewish Residential Services and with Rodef Shalom Congregation, who drew upon her for guidance in displaying its own works of religious art. Other organizations she served include the National Council of Jewish Women, Pittsburgh Section, and the Jewish Federation of Greater Pittsburgh.

Well into her '80s, Jane was still climbing ladders to work on her larger pieces, still seeking adventure and inspiration in travel, still acting as mentor to promising young talent, still writing letters to the editor, advocating for the arts.

On the outside Jane projected serenity and a gentle nature; but at her core was an iron will and fierce drive to fulfill her ambitions and perfect her art.

SOURCES:

Jane Haskell: Drawing in Light, by Vicky A. Clark and Melissa Hiller, 2015, American Jewish Museum of the Jewish Community Center of Greater Pittsburgh

Haskell, Jane, oral history interviews, 1994, *Pittsburgh and Beyond: the Experience of the Jewish Community*, National Council of Jewish Women, Pittsburgh Section, Oral History Collection at the University of Pittsburgh (http://images.library.pitt.edu/cgi-bin/i/image/image-idx?view=entry;cc=ncjw;entryid=x-ais196440.189)

Jane Haskell Collection, MSS #1046, Rauh Jewish Archives, Thomas and Katherine Detre Library and Archives, Senator John Heinz History Center

Irene Loewenthal Jacob

(April 20, 1928–December 6, 2012)

by Carol Stein Bleier

I rene (pronounced Irenee) Loewenthal Jacob, horticulturist, was inspired by a lifelong interest in gardening to establish the largest biblical garden in North America. A deep love of Judaism and a curiosity about plants in the ancient world created the desire to research biblical roots in nature. Along with her husband, Rabbi Walter Jacob, Irene traveled widely and found few biblical gardens, which led them to design in 1987 Rodef Shalom Congregation's Biblical Botanical Garden in Pittsburgh, Pa., where Rabbi Jacob was then Senior Rabbi.

(photograph courtesy of Rodef Shalom Congregation Archives)

The youngest of three children, Irene was born on April 20, 1928 in Hamburg, Germany to Ludwig Loewenthal, an insurance broker, and Hannah, a homemaker. Her family, which included siblings Eli and Eva, was close-knit and observant, and life was normal until the growing threat of Nazism and signs of increasing anti-Semitism adversely impacted their lives. This was especially evident in 1936 when Irene and her family were vacationing at a seaside resort and were surrounded by Nazi hoodlums. The family dashed to the train station and successfully made it home. Irene's father, traveling in Holland on business, however, saw the worsening situation for the Jews and sensed the impending war getting closer. In the summer of 1938, a few months before Kristallnacht, he took his family quickly out of Germany where they left most of their possessions and immigrated to England.

Irene grew up in wartime London with her family sharing a small house with several relatives who had also fled Nazism. Among the relatives was her nine-year old cousin Walter, whom she would later marry. Irene learned English, and after leaving school at the age of 16, she apprenticed in a large nursery. She did secretarial work for her father and then joined the staff of the Friends of Hebrew University, and then the immigration department at the Jewish Agency, where she met future leaders of Israel as they visited London. She often took people on tours of London. One time she gave a tour for the Austrian-born Jewish philosopher Martin Buber and his daughter. Watching the development of Israel, and following her brother, she moved to Israel in 1948. She stayed initially on a kibbutz but after battling rats one night, she was convinced that kibbutz life was not for her. She trained as a radiology technician and worked in several large hospitals.

As a volunteer, Irene Jacob (second from right) created and managed the docent program at Phipps Conservatory and Botanical Gardens. She used the experience to create a similar program at the Biblical Botanical Garden at Rodef Shalom. She is seen here with the first class of docents at Phipps and Mayor Richard S. Caliguiri. (photograph courtesy of Phipps Conservatory and Botanical Gardens)

When she moved to Tel Aviv, she rented a rooftop apartment and had her first real garden. On a vacation to visit England in 1958 she stopped in Rome and became reacquainted with her cousin Walter, whom she had not seen for two decades. They were engaged after a week, married in five weeks, and Irene moved to Pittsburgh to join her husband.

Life in Pittsburgh for Irene was busy, filled with duties as a rebbetzin, and her varied interests. Her innate enthusiasm, an air of adventure, and the ability to see and solve problems resulted in many serious projects with beneficial outcomes. She established a Mother's Day Out program at Rodef Shalom Temple, trained as a docent at the Carnegie Museum, then formed a docent program at Phipps Conservancy and

One goal of the Biblical Botanical Garden was to give visitors a better understanding of the role of plants in the lives of ancient peoples. To that end, Irene Jacob produced a summer newsletter called *PapyruS* that combined information about the garden with new research and scholarship. (documents courtesy of Rodef Shalom Congregation Archives)

PapyruS

A Publication of the Rodef Shalom Biblical Botanical Garden
Irene Jacob - Editor - Volume 6, Number 1, June 1994

THE AGELESS ART OF DYEING
Colors from Nature from the Bible to the Present

The Exhibit

What would our lives be like without the use of dyes? The love of bright colors has a long history and is interwoven with the fabric of our lives.

The language of color has enabled us to express our feelings and emotions, such as happiness, grief or love. Color symbolism differs from one society to another and may even depict opposite emotions.

Our exhibit will deal with plant dyes. The art of extracting colors sytematically from plants originated in China and India and passed to Babylon and Assyria, from where it passed to Egypt. Earlier, primitive people used crushed leaves, flowers, berries, and bark of trees; such colors soon faded.

We possess a great deal of multicolored material from ancient Egypt's tombs. The most color drenched coat of Biblical times must be Joseph's coat. When Moses led the Jews from Egypt, they carried with them the knowledge of dyes. "And they made upon the skirts of the robe pomegranates of blue, purple and scarlet and twined linen" (Ex 39:24).

Decorated objects, such as pottery and clothing have been discovered in many archaeological excavations. The ancient craftsmen carefully guarded the secrets of their profession, so what remains concealed still far exceeds what we know. Ancient writers recorded that there were once nearly a thousand different sources of natural dyes, but because of the secrecy surrounding their recipes, many of them have been lost forever. Although it is often extremely difficult to recreate the ancient processes of color production, modern laboratory analysis has enabled scholars to determine the structure of the pigments.

Our exhibit will concentrate on dyes from plants: Indigo and woad for blue; madder for red; weld, safflower, pomegranate, and saffron for yellow; and cutch from acacias for brown. These are among the oldest dye plants known to the Eurasian civilizations.

Lectures

Wednesday, June 8 - Noon - Doris Binstock
INTRODUCTION TO THE GARDEN

Sunday, June 12 - 7 p.m. - Irene Jacob
JOSEPH'S COAT OF MANY COLORS
What Were They?

Other Pittsburgh Gardens

When you visit our Garden, we would like to introduce you to neighboring gardens which you may enjoy. We have prepared a guide which will provide instructions on how to reach Phipps Conservatory, the Pittsburgh Civic Garden Center, the gardens and conservatory of the Frick Art and History Center, as well as the Hunt Botanical Library. Create your own garden tour and start with us.

Ancient Israel will be the subject of this issue. Egypt and Mesopotamia will be discussed in the July and August newsletters.

Color in Ancient Israel
by Walter Jacob

Color as a concept is not part of the common vocabulary of the Hebrew Bible. The term *beromim* (Ezekiel 27.24) comes from the Akkadian *birmu* (color). In Ezekiel it is used for colored garments. A separate term for color came into general usage only in *Mishnaic* Hebrew (200 C.E.).

The best known Biblical passages which deal with dyes described the ancient desert tabernacle which was the site of Israelite worship during the forty year sojourn in the desert and the early centuries in Canaan. The tent and courtyard have been described in great detail in Exodus. The linens used were dyed blue, purple, and scarlet (Ex 26.1-3, 31, 36). Ram skins were dyed red (Ex 26.14; 40.19).

The garments of the priests were of fine linen white or dyed blue, purple and scarlet (Ex 28.2 - 6). At other times only "weaver's colors" were specified (Ex 28.39, 40, 42). The *Ephod* was blue and its skirt were decorated with pomegranates of blue, purple and scarlet as well as golden bells (Ex 28.31-35); while the breastplate had valuable stones sewn into it (Ex 28.19-30).

Many other Biblical texts refer to colored objects, as for example, Joseph's coat (Gen 37.3). The prophetic books also also contain many incidental reference to the use of dyes, such as Ezekiel's reference to trade in colored garments with Tarshish (Ezekiel 27.24).

Archeologists have discovered colored textiles in Judean caves dating from 6500 B.C.E. Slightly later textiles with green, red, black, tan, and yellow were used. In addition colored pottery, wall decorations, and cosmetics from the Biblical period have been discovered. Dyes came from plants, animals and minerals.

In pre-historic times hundreds of dye materials were used; only the best among them survived once broader trading began. We know nothing of ancient dye techniques as these were closely guarded craft secrets. Reports of "recipe" papyri exist only from later Hellenistic times (200 B.C.E.)

Talmudic Dyeing

Indigo

Both the Jerusalem and Babylonian Talmud indicate that the craft of dyeing was highly considered. Those who practised it were identified through a badge of colored wool worn behind the ear. Jewish and Syrian dyers were considered the best in the Roman Empire. A number of dye factories have been excavated in ancient Israel at Tel Dor and in other locations.

Color without Dyes

A simple way of obtaining color in wool was the careful sorting of brown, red, white or black strands. The natural colors of sheep, goat, and camel wool were interwoven and at times also with linen, although this was prohibited (Lev 19.19). Such clothes have been found in various Israeli sites. This technique was also used in striped designs which have been found in Egyptian tombs.

Painting colors, both organic and inorganic onto cloth was another possibility. As there was no binder between the pigment and the cloth, this usually did not last.

Organic Dyes

It was possible to color textiles through various minerals, but the best shades of color which remained fast came from organic sources. Wool proved to be easier to dye than linen as its chemical structure is denser. We will list the most popular colors and some of the plant sources.

BLUE - All plants utilized produced the indigotin, a dark blue powder. Fairly sophisticated techniques were necessary for the dyeing process.

Woad (*Isatis tinctoria*) is a temperate climate biennial and perennial plant from 2 to 5 feet high with lanceolate leaves from which the blue dye is obtained. It grows a rosette from 6 to 18 inches in diameter, depending on soil with stems 2-3 feet high. The leaves are small and the plant produces yellow flowers and a large number of purplish brown seeds. The plant grows quickly. Each plant may produce half a pound of leaves over a season. Two pounds of leaves will provide dye for four ounces of fibers. The name woad is derived from Anglo-Saxon "wad" and may be the source of our term "weed".

True Indigo (*Indigofera tinctoria*) is a tropical 3 to 5 feet high shrub with oval leaves from which the dye is extracted; they contain thirty times as much dye as woad. The plant could be grown in Israel, but it seems that most of the dye was imported in cakes from Persia, India and Arabia.

Clothes of Egyptian mummies show that they may have been dyed with indigo as early as 3000 B.C.E. Indigo was not widely used in ancient times as woad was much cheaper and more accessible. Romans used it more for coloring items other than textiles, for wall paintings, shields, and also made ink from it which they called indicum.

Blue was also derived from more than fifty other species which contain indigotin. They were used locally while the dye industry used Indigo and Woad. In the Hellenistic period both plants were seriously cultivated and Palestine and Syria were renowned for their dye techniques.

RED - Madder (*Rubia tinctorum*) was the principal source of red. The dye is produced through fermentation of the root. The dye has been found in Egypt and Israel from 2500 B.C.E. onward.

RED/SCARLET was derived from several Kermes species of the coccid insects (*Kermes biblicus, vermilio,* and *palestiniensis*). The insects feed on the oak (*Quercus coccifera*) which may have grown in ancient Israel. The tree was introduced to Assyria in 1100 B.C.E. for the sake of the dye. This was the *tola-at shani* of Exodus.

PURPLE/BLUE may have been produced from mixing red and blue, but the best source was a class of sea snails (*Murex brandaris, Murex trunculus,* and *Thais haemastoma*). *Tekhelet* and *argaman* of Exodus were produced from the glands of snails. The process was fairly sophisticated and a large number of snails had to be harvested. This was developed into a major industry by the Phoenicians in Tyre and the color came to be known as Tyranean Purple.

YELLOW - Safflower (*Carthamus tinctorius*)

produces a flower with red and yellow petals. When an alkaline substance is used, a pinkish red will be produced while water will produce a yellow dye.

Saffron (*Crocus sativus*) is a fall blooming corm, which goes dormant in spring. This perennial plant is propagated by daughter corms formed on the mother corm. 4 to 6 flowers are produced per plant and then the plant dies. The three stigmas and part of the styles constitute in its dry state, the pure saffron of commerce. Powdered saffron is dark orange-red. The powder imparts a yellow color to water. Because the stigmas are not allowed to fulfill their organic function, the cultivated crocus is sterile.

Weld (*Reseda luteola*) is a tall annual, native to the entire Mediterranean. The flowers are borne on erect spikes. All part of the plant, except the roots are used.

Pomegranate (*Punica granatum*) is a small tree found throughout the Mediterranean world. It may attain a height of 6 feet. The skin of the fruit is used, especially for dyeing leather

The Yellow Jew's Badge

Yellow, the color taken from the precious saffron (*Crocus sativus*) was to become the color of persecution for Jews for almost 2,000 years - till the "yellow star" of Nazi times. This occurred despite the lofty status of saffron colored garments in earlier periods when the saffron crocus was an important item in trade. That began in ancient times in Asia Minor and spread throughout the Mediterranean. The word crocus is of Greek origin, saffron is derived from the Arabic word *zafaran* - yellow.

Yellow was the most important color after purple as the color of majesty and enjoyed special attention from the Egyptians, who dyed mummy cloths with it. Saffron was mentioned in the Song of Songs (4.14) as *karkom* and Jews used it for dyeing cloths - the dye was found on textiles of the Bar Kochba period in the Cave of Letters. The ancient Phoenicians dedicated saffron cakes to the goddess Astarte.

Saffron was the principal yellow dye of Greeks and Romans and it was, at one time, the official color.

Cleopatra used saffron in her cosmetics. For Hindus and Muslims it has always been important in worship. It was used as caste markings and to color ceremonial garmentsas well as bridal veils; Muslim divines used a saffron extract to write charms.

Later the Florentines used its blossoms on their coat of arms, another indication of its value as an item of trade. The color was considered a symbol of royalty until it was assumed by the most refined prostitutes, the *hetaerae*.

Its use as a designation for Jews began under the Muslim ruler, Omar (634 C.E.) who legislated that Jews wear a yellow patch. In 1200 this was changed to include all Jews, who had converted to Islam; they were required to wear yellow clothing. It was later used to distinguish Jews from the rest of the population and to mock them. A yellow saffron patch had to be worn by Jews in Prague (1067), Navarra (1234), in France (1269) in England (1275), Portugal (1325), Augsburg (1434), Regensburg (1452), Bamberg and Nurnberg (1451), Elsass (1547), Austria (1551), Worms (1557), Frankfurt (1614), Leipzig (1682). While a yellow hat was forced upon Jews in Marseille, Venice, Verona and Rome during various decades from the 13th to the 16th century.

We should note, on the other hand, that saffron was an important item of Jewish spice traders through much of the Middle Ages. This was especially true in Northern Europe.

The Saffron Industry Then and Now

The highest grade of saffron still comes from Spain where it was introduced by Arabs in the 10th century. It grows best in rich, well-drained sandy or loamy soil with adequate rainfall. Every four years the corms are dug, cleaned and set in another plot, allowing the depleted ground to lie fallow for ten years.

The work of harvesting is back-breaking; the petals must be picked before sun rise and within hours of coming into full bloom. The crocus only blooms for 15 days. The stigmas are handpicked daily, just as the flowers open. The flowers must be stripped on the day that is is harvested. At the next stage the filaments are roasted and stored in moisture proof containers for an indefinite period, so it "is like money in the bank." No machinery can duplicate the gentleness of hand harvesting.

As saffron production is labor intensive, it is expensive . About 210,000 dried stigmas from 70,000 flowers are required for one pound of true saffron. An ounce requires 4,300 flowers. During the Renaissance a pound of saffron would buy a horse. The expensive process and the temptation to adulterate the final product had already been noted by Pliny in the first century. Saffron was adulterated with calendula, marigold, safflower, logwood, brazilwood, the silk of corn, poppy, outer skin of red onions (cut to suitable size) and in modern times with aniline dyes and synthetic pigments.

Saffron today is primarily used to color and flavor foods such as cheese, butter, pastry and confectionery. Its medicinal use is now disputed.

Tropicals and Cold June Nights

Our tropical plants such as sugar, castor bean and many others continue to grow very slowly due to the cool nights in late May and early June. Many other plants have also been affected and we hope to see them grow later in the summer.

Our Garden Books

THE HEALING PAST *Pharmaceuticals in the Biblical and Rabbinic World* edited by Irene and Walter Jacob (E.J.Brill, Leiden, 1993, 126 pp., ISBN 90 04 09643 4), presents the papers of our international symposium on ancient medicine in Egypt, Israel, Mesopotamia, and early Rabbinic Judaism. It has been published as part of *Studies in Ancient Medicine*.

BIBLICAL PLANTS *A Guide to the Rodef Shalom Biblical Botanical Garden*, Irene Jacob, (Pittsburgh, 1989, 60 pp. Illustrated, ISBN 0-929699-01-7). This guide describes the Biblical plants as well as their ancient and modern uses. It is profusely illustrated. Plant names are given in English, Hebrew, German, French and Italian.

Published by the
Rodef Shalom Biblical Botanical Garden
4905 5th Avenue
Pittsburgh, PA 15213
412-621-6566 FAX 412-621-5475

Botanical Gardens. As Education Coordinator at Phipps, she initiated a small winter exhibition there on biblical plants. She had a strong interest in music, played the violin, accordion, and recorder, and formed the Pittsburgh Recorder Society.

Irene and Walter raised three children, Claire, Kenney, and Danny. When their seriously handicapped daughter needed long-term living facilities as she got older, Irene and Walter, as they had done so many times before, saw a dire need and filled it. A three-year effort with major battles that included endless hearings before state authorities and County Council resulted in the first group home in Western Pennsylvania, Horizon Homes, now Mainstay Life Services, the largest residential service provider in Allegheny County. The site of the first group home had an outdoor and indoor garden, which Irene and Walter tended.

Irene's major interest and passion was learning, teaching, and writing about plants and gardens. For a decade, she had a business, "The Plant Hunter," designing indoor and outdoor gardens. She and her husband visited more than a thousand gardens in North America as well as archeological sites and museums, and wrote half a dozen books on biblical plants. Not seeing some of the gardens because there was not any guidebook to direct them, they wrote their own, *Gardens of North America and Hawaii, A Traveler's Guide*. They were fortunate to have the opportunity to create their biblical garden on a third of an acre adjacent to Temple Rodef Shalom. Irene shaped the garden to replicate Israel and included a waterfall, desert, stream, a representation of the River Jordan, two bridges, a pavilion, and walkways. During their travels they visited obscure nurseries bringing home different biblical plants, devoting time and effort to make sure the plants survived in the cold Pittsburgh climate. In the winter most of the plants went to a greenhouse, though Irene took the most fragile plants out of the ground and brought them into their home. Among the plants she cultivated, studied and researched were those used for food and medicine.

As the garden developed, new programs and exhibits with a theme related to biblical times were planned yearly, with educational materials, guest lecturers, symposia and the informational journal *PapyruS* that Irene published three times each summer. Several thousand visitors from all across America, Europe and Asia visit each season.

Irene was honored by WQED Television with the Vita Award, the Men's Garden Club, and the Pennsylvania Museum Council. She lectured on the history of gardens and other horticultural subjects throughout the United States. Irene became interested in ethnobotany and was recruited to teach it at Chatham College (now Chatham University). She also taught at the University of Pittsburgh and Community College of Allegheny County. She wrote articles for encyclopedias, magazines and newspapers. Her published books include *Biblical Plants, Botanical Symbols in World Religions, Plants of the Bible and Their Uses* as well as several more that she co-authored.

Rabbi Jacob gave a moving tribute to his wife on the occasion of her death on December 6, 2012 saying, "Irene led a life filled with a sense of purpose and a wish to create beauty. Eighty-five years, one could be satisfied and she was. Both she and I have ever been mindful that but for a twist of fate - we and our families would long ago have become a wisp of smoke in the dark skies of Poland. We were among the fortunate ones who came to this blessed land America, and this good and friendly city."

SOURCES:

Pursuing Peace Across the Alleghenies: The Rodef Shalom Congregation, 1856-2005. Walter Jacob, Editor, 2005.

Gardening From The Bible to North America: Essays in Honor of Irene Jacob. Walter Jacob, Editor, 2005.

Jacob, Irene, oral history interviews, 1999, *Pittsburgh and Beyond: the Experience of the Jewish Community,* National Council of Jewish Women, Pittsburgh Section, Oral History Collection at the University of Pittsburgh (http://images.library.pitt.edu/cgi-bin/i/image/image-idx?view=entry;cc=ncjw;entryid=x-ais196440.206)

Sally Kalson

(October 21, 1950–September 27, 2014)

by Eric Lidji

E very city longs for a native son or daughter who can speak on its behalf. In Pittsburgh, it was Sally Kalson. Born and raised in western Pennsylvania, she spent nearly 40 years as a journalist, covering issues of importance to the city and the world.

Kalson came from a family that was both illustrative and commonplace. Her grandfather Harry Kalson immigrated to Pittsburgh from Kovno, in present-day Lithuania, in 1891. He worked as a plumber and building contractor before starting Kalson's Bath House, a much-needed institution in the Hill District in the days before household plumbing was ubiquitous.

(photograph courtesy of the Kalson family)

The business made him prominent in the community. In 1907, he was elected to the Common Council, a wild and often dysfunctional forerunner of the current city council. He helped found Montefiore Hospital and Tifereth Israel Congregation, where he was president for nine years. He was also president of the short-lived United Orthodox Congregations of Pittsburgh.

Kalson's maternal grandmother, Eva Gold Friedman, was born in Pittsburgh to parents who had emigrated from Vilna Gubernia, in Lithuania. She raised four children with an open-heartedness that Kalson once described in a memorial column: "Mrs. Friedman's main occupation was matriarch, which she believed meant the free distribution of unconditional love." Kalson's parents, Bill and Edna Belle Kalson, met at the Laurel Y Camp, shortly after World War II. Bill Kalson had studied to be an engineer but was unable to surmount discriminatory

In addition to her newspaper work, Sally Kalson was an avid outdoorswoman. (photograph courtesy of the Kalson family)

hiring practices in the industry and went back to school to become a lawyer. Edna Kalson had a knack for writing and music and became a well-known presence in the Jewish community, particularly at Jewish Family & Children's Services, where she worked for many years.

Sally Kalson was the middle of three children. She graduated from Mt. Lebanon High School and then the University of Pittsburgh with a degree in speech and communication. Her first job in the newspaper business was a three-year stint at the *Jewish Chronicle* of Pittsburgh, where she organized the social calendars for Jewish groups, reviewed books and wrote feature articles on a variety of topics, including the impacts of the Yom Kippur War and efforts to save Soviet Jewry. Among her first pieces for the newspaper was a review of the Holocaust-themed children's novel *When Hitler Stole Pink Rabbit.* Kalson criticized the author for diminishing the Jewishness of her characters, although she acknowledged one small benefit to this approach: "A Jewish child who has been raised learning about the Holocaust can also learn that, while Hitler specialized in anti-Semitism, his crime was against all humanity." This ability to draw broad lessons from specific experiences would become a hallmark of her later work.

After leaving the *Chronicle,* Kalson was briefly the public relations director of Tri-State Israel Bonds before taking a job at the short-lived *Pittsburgher Magazine* and then working for *Pennsylvania Illustrated* in Harrisburg. She soon returned to Pittsburgh to become a freelancer for publications such as the *New York Times Magazine* and to teach journalism at Chatham College (now Chatham University). In late 1983, she compiled a special report on Jewish poverty in the region for the United Jewish Federation titled, "Jews on the Edge: How

Sally Kalson started her journalism career at the *Jewish Chronicle* shortly out of college and eventually became well known as a columnist for the *Pittsburgh Post-Gazette.* These two articles from either end of her career show the consistency of her insight, clarity and strong opinions. The first, from the January 20, 2013 issue of the *Post-Gazette,* shows her skills at mixing personal and political ideas. The second, from the March 15, 1973 issue of the *Jewish Chronicle,* shows how she brought her personal beliefs to a simple book review. (documents courtesy of the *Pittsburgh Post-Gazette* and the Pittsburgh Jewish Newspaper Project).

SALLY KALSON

The world before Roe

Women will get abortions; the question is whether they can do so safely

My mother is 91 and matriarch of three subsequent generations. For the first 51 years of her life, abortion was outlawed in this country. Desperate women with unwanted pregnancies would resort to all manner of dangerous terminations, sometimes ruining their wombs for future pregnancies or dying from bleeding, shock or sepsis.

On Jan. 22, 1973, the Supreme Court legalized abortion in Roe v. Wade. Shortly thereafter, sterile clinics and hospitals replaced dirty basements. Medical professionals replaced quacks and Clorox. Abortion seekers became patients, not criminals. The result was a near-end to women dying from preventable complications.

The other result, of course, was more abortions — or so we surmise, since the illegal ones weren't counted — roughly 1.2 million each year at this point. It's safe to assume that many of those would not have taken place if women still feared for their lives in the process.

With the 40th anniversary of Roe a few days away, I asked Mom for her thoughts on the subject.

"I thought legalization was long overdue," she said. "It's a private matter. People can use their own beliefs as their guide, but it doesn't belong in politics. I always felt that, and I still do."

But as we all know, politics began overtaking abortion from the moment Roe was decided. The ruling sparked an epic battle that continues to this day over when life begins and who gets to decide the answer. The past 40 years have seen no end of marches, organizing and fundraising for and against legal abortion, as foes chip away at women's constitutional right and advocates fight back.

The two sides have argued over terminology ("late-term" vs. "partial birth"), medical science (foes falsely linking abortion to breast cancer) and birth control (religious leaders labeling some methods as abortifacients).

Anti-abortion groups set up fake clinics where they could talk women out of the procedure (today they're more up front about their true mission). Protesters chained themselves to doors, picketed with gory photos and accosted patients at clinic entrances. A more virulent strain of the movement threatened clinic staff, bombed facilities and murdered doctors, one of them at church.

Meanwhile, ultrasounds brought fetal development into the open, and neonatal medicine made life viable at ever-earlier stages. The technology affected the public's evolving views, especially on second- and third-trimester abortions — about 12 percent of terminations, according to the Guttmacher Institute.

In addition, the stigma of single motherhood began to fade. Some religious groups that had shipped pregnant girls out to the hinterlands in shame shifted to running maternity homes in town.

As legal challenges to Roe failed to overturn it, the battle lines moved elsewhere. Doctors at Catholic hospitals reported being forced to sacrifice patient care to church teachings. Some pharmacists refused to dispense the morning-after pill, and some employers protested a birth-control mandate in medical coverage for workers.

An increasingly militant right wing has been driving onerous state regulations designed solely to limit access — repeated visits, longer waiting periods, invasive tests with no medical value and, as in Pennsylvania, costly renovations that have forced some clinics to close.

"This past year has been a real challenge," said Becky McDermott, executive director of Allegheny Reproductive Health Care in East Liberty, which spent $200,000 to comply with new requirements. "But women still need us and we're still here," she added.

Then there are the efforts to strip funding from Planned Parenthood, the nation's leading provider of reproductive health care and birth control, especially for poor women. Only 3 percent of its services involve abortion, but that's enough to make it a right-wing target. Since 2010, nine states have tried to defund the organization, only to be told that doing so will cost them millions in federal funding.

Texas Gov. Rick Perry, however, remains undaunted. He is forfeiting hundreds of millions in Medicaid dollars rather than include Planned Parenthood in the Texas Women's Health Program. A federal appeals judge upheld the ban last week, and now 50,000 women, many of them poor, have to find another place for free breast cancer screenings, pap smears and birth control. If they can.

The further we get from botched illegal abortions, the easier it is for right-wing pols to take concern for women and girls out of the picture. Every punitive law shifts focus from protecting women's health to controlling their bodies and punishing their behavior.

Reading this list, you'd think the public had turned against legal abortion, but it hasn't. A recent Gallup Poll showed that 77 percent of Americans believe abortion should remain legal in some or all circumstances.

"Women aren't asking politicians for advice on mammograms or any other kind of health care, and they don't want them involved in this either," said Kim Evert, director of Planned Parenthood of Western Pennsylvania.

"It's hard to believe we're back here, talking about contraception and rape," said Claire Keyes, who ran Allegheny Reproductive for three decades before retiring four years ago. "The idea that women need to let men make the decisions about their bodies is so degrading and enraging.

"Women have always been the prime deciders of when and if a new life comes into the world through their bodies," she continued. "You're never, ever going to stop abortion. It'll just be less accessible and more dangerous as women have to jump through more hoops."

Reactionary forces won't be satisfied until abortion once again makes women fear for their lives. That's why, 40 years after Roe, we need to remember what that world looked like and why we can't go back.

Sally Kalson is a columnist for the Post-Gazette (skalson@post-gazette.com, 412-263-1610).

Adar II 11, 5733   Thursday March 15, 1973   The Jewish Chronicle of Pittsburgh-11

The People and
The Book

Kerr Won't Face Judaism

"WHEN HITLER STOLE PINK RABBIT", by Judith Kerr, drawings by the author. Coward, McCann and Geoghegan, Inc., 191 p.p. $4.95

Reviewed By SALLY KALSON, Chronicle Staff Writer

Anna was nine years old and very proud of her famous father. After all, he wrote for the biggest newspapers and magazines in Berlin, and everyone thought he was important. But lately, he and her mother had mysteriously taken to lecturing her about her religion, even though they had never gone to temple. Anna barely knew what "Jewish" meant.

Suddenly her father was gone, and she found her family sneaking out of Berlin to join him in Switzerland, leaving behind house, toys and even her favorite uncle. She was officially a refugee. It was 1933.

Thus "Judith Kerr begins "When Hitler Stole Pink Rabbit", based on her own childhood. It is a story not so much of a Jewish family as of a family that just happens to be Jewish. They never really come to grips with their Jewish identity, even though they are forced out of their country because of it. Still, Kerr's account of the moves from Germany to Switzerland, France and England and all the adjustments in between, makes for a charming children's book.

The author has a way of capturing those things that make childhood an adventure. In spite of all the uncertainty of leaving her homeland for a strange place, Anna is excited by the idea. "To be in a strange country where everything is different-to live in a different house, go to a different school with different children-a huge urge to experience it all overcame her."

Experience it she does: from an almost fatal dose of influenza her first month in Switzerland to a frustrating struggle with a new language in France. She is chased home from school by a group of boys pummeling her with stones, only to discover they are proclaiming their love. She is ostracized by her playmates when a rich family comes to visit. All this is coupled with the additional puzzlement of growing up. But she survives with even more determination to become a "good refugee."

Author Kerr acknowledges the fact that what appears adventuresome to a child can be grim to an adult. Anna's parents, while encouraging their children to adjust, must face the reality of having lost a homeland, and of having to be poor for the first time in their lives.

Kerr lets us know she is dealing with real people who have real shortcomings and weaknesses, something too often ignored by children's books. Even the most tightly knit family car begin to show signs of strain when it feels alone and un

CENTRAL figures from Judith Kerr's children's book make ready for another move.

JUDITH KERR
A Child's Eye View.

certain in a strange land. It hurts Anna to see her worried mother and impractical father quarreling over the use of their last few francs. But the family is fortunate to make new friends who help relieve the strain.

It must be noted here that the family's Judaism seems rather unsubstantiated throughout the book. They leave Germany not so much because they are Jews as because freedom of speech and press is threatened. They celebrate Christmas with Christmas spirit-there is no mention of Hanuka. According to Anna, "being Jewish was just something you were because your parents and grandparents are Jewish."

There are two incidents that tell her differently. She makes friends with visiting children who are lots of fun until their parents fill them with marijhana. In France, the landlady is nice enough until they are one day late with the rent; then she spits some choice antisemitic remarks at them. Anna learns about people from these incidents but not about being Jewish. She begins to see what ugly terms human nature can take, but does not relate it to her Judaism.

Still, there is something to be said for this treatment. A Jewish child who has been raised learning about the Holocaust can also learn that, while Hitler specialized in antisemitism, his crime was against all humanity.

'House Tour 1'
To Show Katz
Art Collection

On March 26, 1973, WIIC-TV will present a special program entitled House Tour #1. The 30-minute show which will air at 12:30 p.m. is a personally conducted view of the art treasures in the Pittsburgh and New York apartments of Mr. and Mrs. Joseph M. Katz.

Mr. Katz, who is chairman and president of Papercraft Corporation, which he founded in 1945, has for many years been a collector of modern painting and sculpture.

According to Mr. Katz "I can collect art because these objects give me, as nothing else can, a sense of total tranquility."

Rabbi Rosenberg to Key United Synagogue Parley

The keynote address at the Conference of the Western Pa. Region of United Synagogue will be delivered by Rabbi Yaakov G. Rosenberg, spiritual leader of Congregation Adath Jeshurun, Elkins Park, Pa.

Rabbi Rosenberg was graduated from Johns Hopkins University, Baltimore Hebrew College, and was

RABBI YAAKOV ROSENBERG
Serves AJCongress

ordained by the Jewish Theological Seminary. He has just been re-elected to the Board of Philadelphia's Federation of Jewish Agencies and currently serves on the National Chairman of the Commission on Jewish Affairs of the American Jewish Congress, and is a member of the National Rabbinic Cabinet of the Seminary.

Mrs. Harriet Kruman, chairman of the Conference on "The Role and Status of Women in Conservative Judaism", urged community participation.

The Conference will be held at Congregation Beth El of South Hills, 1900 Cochran Road on Sunday, March 25. Cost for the brunch and all sessions is $5 or $1.50 for sessions only. For reservations or information, call the Regional Executive Director, David Dinkin, at 521-6788, or Mrs. Kruman at 683-2937. Dr. David L. Chamovitz of Aliquippa is President of the Region.

Schedule for the Conference: 11 to 12, Registration; 12 to 1:30, Brunch and Keynote Address; 1:30 to 3:30 Workshops; 3:30 to 4, Coffee Break; 4 to 5, Summations and Open Discussion.

worry less
SMILE MORE!

start saving today... the GUARANTY way
$2,000-1 Year Savings Certificates
5¾% Per Annum
6% annual yield
GUARANTY
INSURED   SAVINGS
5857 Forbes Ave.
In Squirrel Hill

WANTED:
Spring and Summer, Clothing and House Furnishing to Sell on Consignment. Good Condition. Will Pick Up.
THE KLOTHES KLOSET
109 Mayran Ave., Oakland   682-9911

OFFICIAL STATE INSPECTION CENTER
TIRES
INSPECTION $4.50
NOBODY UNDERSELLS US
MARTY WIKES
BONUS TIRE CENTER
6200 Saltsburg Road, Penn Hills • 795-1775

Pre-eminent!
Sander L. Lenenberg of Pittsburgh

To be pre-eminent is to be truly outstanding. It describes the 1972 performance of Sander L. Lenenberg of Pittsburgh. By arranging for more than $8 million of new coverage for his clients, Mr. Lenenberg, for the second year in succession, led all Great-West Life representatives in the United States and Canada in 1972. This is his fourth consecutive year as the sales leader for the United States and the third time in his four-year association with Great-West that he has been the international leader. Quite an achievement!

Sander Lenenberg has developed his extensive clientele on the strength of professional competence, dedication to service, and a special talent for business insurance and estate planning. Great-West Life congratulates its 1972 sales leader!

Great-West Life
ASSURANCE COMPANY

Sander Lenenberg's office is Suite 3121, One Oliver Plaza. Telephone 281-3500.

Close to Home is Trouble?" She was a long-standing member of Congregation Dor Hadash in Squirrel Hill. In later years, she chaired JFilm, a local Jewish film festival.

Kalson joined the staff of the *Pittsburgh Post-Gazette* in 1982 as a general assignment reporter, covering suburban politics and criminal trials. She also wrote features, including some on Jewish themes, such as a profile of a local matchmaker. Her career changed dramatically in 1984, after she began writing for the relatively new "Saturday Diary" feature of the *Post-Gazette*. The loose, personal format drew out her voice as a commentator. She railed against fads and hypocrisies in a frank and humorous fashion, such as one controversial column attacking a government initiative promoting the "rhythm method" as an effective birth control technique in the Third World. "The concept, you can see, is dazzling in its myriad applications," she wrote. "Human-rights violations? Don't get tortured. Election fraud? Don't vote. Slum housing? Don't live indoors. Rat infestation? Don't get bitten. Apartheid? Don't be black." In time, the *Post-Gazette* made Kalson a regular columnist and also gave her the opportunity to tackle larger topics such as capricious judges and controversial public art projects. In time, she also earned spots as a regular commentator on local radio and television stations.

Kalson gracefully shifted her attentions between her work and her home. She postponed her 1988 wedding several times to accommodate a murder trial she was covering and filed columns from home while on maternity leave. She regularly wrote about her family, including her husband Ed Feinstein, her daughter Zoe, her mother Edna Belle Kalson, and her "nana" Eva Friedman.

During the 1990s and 2000s, Kalson established herself as a voice of social consciousness in Pittsburgh. She gave considerable attention to issues important to women and girls, such as birth control and abortion, Title IX and the sexism she saw underlying political coverage. Following a diagnosis of ovarian cancer at age 52, her specific combination of reporting, candor and humanity reached its fullest form. She regularly detailed the insights and humiliations of chemotherapy and cancer treatment. She praised her nurses and doctors. But she took aim at the University of Pittsburgh Medical Center, which she felt was abusing its tax-exempt status by fighting with rival health-care providers, paying excessive salaries to top management, outsourcing working-class and middle-class jobs and fighting with unions and labor groups. In one of her most famous and often-quoted columns, from December 2011, in the midst of one of many treatments, she wrote: "I wonder if UPMC President Jeffrey Romoff would like to come down from his penthouse and inhabit my world for the next few months. Maybe then he'd see the colossal folly of threatening to separate me and millions of others from affordable access to trusted medical providers when we're already holding on by our fingernails. The last thing I need in the midst of aching and retching and sleepless nights contemplating my own mortality is UPMC's president threatening to price me out of future access to the team that is keeping me alive."

As the daughter, sister and wife of lawyers, Kalson once drew a connection between her profession and that of the men in her life. "Journalists are frustrated at not being able to effect change, and see things they'd like to get involved with. I think we feel that if we had gone into law, we'd get out there and 'do it.' Lawyers sometimes feel frustrated that their efforts 'to do' things are not getting the attention they deserve," she told the *Chronicle* in 1999.

Her desire "to do" came to fruition through the Newspaper Guild of Pittsburgh, which represents editorial employees of the *Post-Gazette*. Through her various positions with the union, she negotiated ten contracts between the guild and the *Post-Gazette*. "Sally was the heart, soul and moral compass of the guild," Newspaper Guild President and *Post-Gazette* reporter Michael Fuoco said in 2014. "In negotiations, I loved sitting next to her, seeing her eyes narrow and fill with fire when a company proposal violated her sense of justice. And then she would thrust and parry with the company with such skill and logic that we all, on both sides of the table, were in awe."

SOURCES:

Harry Kalson obituary, *Jewish Criterion*, June 1, 1928, p. 26-27

"The Life, Love of Nana," Sally Kalson, *Pittsburgh Post-Gazette*, November 11, 1991, p. 21

"Around the Curves," *Y.M.&W.H.A. Weekly*, May 24, 1946, p. 4

"She sallied forth from the Chronicle," Iris M. Sampson, *Jewish Chronicle*, August 26, 1999, p. 12

"Kerr Won't Face Judaism," Sally Kalson, *Jewish Chronicle*, March 15, 1973, p. 11

"Jews on the Edge: How Close to Home is Trouble," Sally Kalson, *Jewish Chronicle*, December 29, 1983, special insert

"Matchmaking tradition alive, well in Pittsburgh," Sally Kalson, *Pittsburgh-Post-Gazette*, April 12, 1982, p. 11

"Saturday Diary," Sally Kalson, *Pittsburgh Post-Gazette*, May 10, 1986, p. 7

"Obituary: Sally Kalson/Incisive, dogged Post-Gazette journalist," Amy McConnell Schaarsmith, *Pittsburgh Post-Gazette*, September 27, 2014 (http://www.post-gazette.com/news/obituaries/2014/09/27/Obituary-Sal...Incisive-dogged-Post-Gazette-journalist/stories/201409230182, accessed May, 13, 2015)

"I'll bargain with God for my life," Sally Kalson, *Pittsburgh Post-Gazette*, December 18, 2011, p. 19

Liliane Kaufmann

(March 6, 1889–September 7, 1952)

by Laura Cherner

L iliane Kaufmann pursued two seemingly unrelated passions with a similar attitude—to broaden the horizons of
her hometown. Her leadership at Montefiore Hospital helped
the institution navigate its growing pains to become an established and recognized contributor to the regional health care
system. Her Vendôme boutique in Kaufmann's Department
Store brought the glamour of Paris to industrial Pittsburgh.

Liliane Kaufmann was raised in the Manchester neighborhood of old Allegheny City, now the North Side of
Pittsburgh. Her father Isaac Kaufmann had followed his
older brother Jacob to Pittsburgh from their native Germany

(photograph courtesy of the Pittsburgh Jewish Newspaper Project)

Liliane Kaufmann (standing) with her husband E.J. Kaufmann (seated right), her mother-in-law Betty Kaufmann (center) with her brother-in-law Oliver Kaufmann. (photograph courtesy of Kaufmann's Department Store Photographs, c1880-2001, MSP# 371, Rauh Jewish Archives, Thomas and Katherine Detre Library and Archives, Senator John Heinz History Center)

in 1869. Together, they started a men's clothing store on the South Side called J. Kaufmann & Brother. With two younger brothers, they moved the business to downtown in 1877, greatly expanded over the following decades and incorporated Kaufmann's Department Store in 1913. A noted philanthropist, Isaac Kaufmann started several communal institutions in memory of his wife, Emma, including the Emma Kaufmann Clinic in Polish Hill and the Emma Farm Association, a forerunner to the Jewish Community Center's Emma Kaufmann Camp.

From an early age, Liliane Kaufmann had a keen interest in becoming more cosmopolitan. She mastered several foreign languages, wore the most modern fashions and even changed the spelling of her name from "Lillian" to the more elegant "Liliane."

In 1909, she married her first cousin, Edgar Kaufmann. The following year, they had their only child, a son also named Edgar. Edgar and Liliane Kaufmann were known as a striking couple; her fashion and taste were a perfect complement to her businessman husband's entrepreneurial charm. They traveled the world and developed an extensive and prominent social network. She was greatly inspired by European culture and often brought back pieces from her travels to spruce up the family's department store. She transformed Kaufmann's unremarkable 11th floor into the lucrative and luxurious Vendôme boutique. Her secretary, Mary Michaely, once said that the image of Kaufmann returning from a European shopping adventure was "like a queen coming home." The shop was among the first in Pittsburgh to sell designer labels from Europe, and its goods, including antique housewares, became a symbol of status for the elites of Pittsburgh.

Though Liliane Kaufmann represented a picture of grace and elegance in society, the unfortunate realities of anti-Semitism in the early 20th century limited her social ambitions. However, she was a brilliant hostess who quickly established her reputation with some of Pittsburgh's most prominent families. The Kaufmann family also developed a friendship with the architect Frank Lloyd Wright, whom they later hired to design Fallingwater, a weekend home on their property on Bear Run, in Fayette County, southeast of Pittsburgh. Though Edgar and Wright notoriously sparred during construction of the famous home, Liliane maintained a good relationship with the architect throughout the process, and even confided in him about the growing troubles in her marriage. In 1951, after Edgar commissioned a new home in Palm Springs, designed by architect Richard Neutra, Liliane wrote to Wright, "I feel sure that by now you will have seen Edgar and will have gathered that the house in Palm Springs will in no sense have anything to do with me. Edgar and I will never share a house. That also means that when he returns I must leave Fallingwater, which is a great sorrow to me. Therefore I have spent the last few weekends motoring about the countryside and I believe I have found a lovely spot in which to build a small house for myself."

Though Fallingwater was a scenic image of perfection from the outside, their private life inside was far from perfect. Edgar was notorious for taking mistresses. Over time, his predilections became increasingly public. Liliane endured these affairs stoically, but the scandal took its toll and she became increasingly withdrawn and depressed in the later years of her life. After missing dinner one night at Fallingwater, Liliane was discovered unconscious in her bedroom. Because of his mistrust of local doctors, Edgar insisted on her being treated in Pittsburgh, two hours away from their home. Liliane died of a sleeping pill overdose on September 7, 1952 at Mercy Hospital, at the age of 63. The official ruling determined her death to be an accident, but many close family members cited her depression over her failing marriage and suggested the possibility of a suicide.

Though often remembered by Pittsburghers for her taste-making prowess, Liliane Kaufmann was also an active figure in community health and wellbeing. She volunteered for the Red Cross during World War I and World War II. She held a fulltime job at Mercy Hospital assisting emergency room nurses and served on several committees of the Catholic hospital over a 10-year period. Most notably, she was the first and only woman to serve as president of the Montefiore Hospital Board of Trustees, a position she held for nine years. Early in her tenure, she saw the institution through a debate over its mission and its future. A segment of the community accused the hospital of drifting from its original principles of helping Jewish doctors and nurses advance in their field and providing Jewish patients with quality care, including kosher meals. Liliane and others wanted Montefiore to be a community hospital "under Jewish auspices." The debate culminated in a four-hour meeting in January 1935 that Kaufmann "admirably handled in a dignified manner," according to a report at the time in a *Jewish Criterion*. In 1944, she and other members of her family launched a $1 million fundraising campaign to build a new residence for nurses on Fifth Avenue in Oakland. After her death, the wing was named the Liliane S. Kaufmann School of Nursing, in her memory.

Through her various endeavors, Liliane Kaufmann sought to make the Jewish community an important contributor to the entire city of Pittsburgh and the city of Pittsburgh an important contributor to the entire country. Her style and business sense won the heart of high society, despite the anti-Semitism of her day. The refined and regal image that the Kaufmanns projected can be credited largely to Liliane's influence. This image allowed a Jewish family to be not only accepted but idolized. Overall, her contributions to the style, health, and society of Pittsburgh left an unforgettable mark.

Within her first year as president of Montefiore Hospital, Liliane Kaufmann faced a major debate over the history and mission of the Jewish hospital. She addressed the matter directly in a two-page report published in the *Jewish Criterion*. (document courtesy of Pittsburgh Jewish Newspaper Project)

Four   THE JEWISH CRITERION   January 11, 1935

Statement of the Montefiore Hospital

The Board of Trustees of the Montefiore Hospital and its administration, feel that interested members of the community have the right to know the facts, in view of criticisms which have been circulated and published recently. We therefore undertake, in as short and concise a manner as possible, to submit the following statement:

ALLEGED ALTERATION IN AIM, SPIRIT AND INTENTION

Our critic makes the charge that the present administration of the hospital has completely altered the aim, spirit and intention of the institution. This is a general charge, easily made. If he had specified what he claims the original aim, spirit and intention were, and what they are today, it would be possible to discuss it. Since he fails to do so, we will be compelled to discuss the matter without the assistance that we might get from having his ideas on the subject.

The first aim of any hospital is the care of the sick—both those patients who are able to pay for such care and those who cannot pay for it—in the best, most modern manner known to medical science. This, of course, includes efficient nurses, the best food, and such other service, social and otherwise, as a hospital is supposed to render. In the mind of anyone at all acquainted with hospital administration, there can be no deviation from this point: THE CARE OF THE SICK IS THE BASIC REASON FOR THE EXISTENCE OF EVERY INSTITUTION KNOWN AS A HOSPITAL.

In addition to this, a hospital should aim to build its medical staff over a period of time, as close as possible to what might be considered perfection. The idea which seems to be dominant in the thinking of our critics, that a hospital is built in order to further the aims of a few doctors and nurses, is completely outworn and obsolete. The record of the Montefiore Hospital in the past five years shows in the most striking fashion that the above aims have been fully carried out.

If our critic had anything else in mind, it is probably connected with his other charges, and it will therefore receive some further consideration in what we have to say on some of his other complaints.

ALLEGED DENIAL OF OPPORTUNITY TO JEWISH DOCTORS AND NURSES

Another charge is that we are denying an opportunity to Jewish doctors and nurses.

The staff of the Montefiore Hospital consists of 130 physicians and surgeons, of whom 120 are Jewish and 10 non-Jewish. In the past five years we have graduated 35 interns who are now practicing physicians—all of them Jewish. We have provided for our doctors additional opportunities for special work through stipend fellowships, in Pathology, Radiology and Out Patient Service. The hospital has opened wide its every facility for the training of the young Jewish doctor, both in medicine and surgery.

Similarly in the field of nursing, in the past five years the hospital has graduated 26 Jewish nurses. It provided facilities for graduate training in hospitals in Chicago and New York for a considerable number of Jewish nurses, and has placed in positions of importance, both from the nursing and administrative point of view, a large number proportionately of these Jewish graduates.

So much for a specific answer to the baseless charges of this man. Before finishing our answer to this charge, we want to call your attention to its ridiculousness. The Hospital Board is composed of men and women who have been devoting considerable of their time and attention to building up and maintaining the hospital. Although they all have their own affairs to look after, they have, nevertheless, devoted the necessary time to the interests of the hospital. They have not, like our critic, any selfish interests to serve. Does it not seem to be the height of absurdity to claim that these men and women, who are taking time from their own affairs to devote to this hospital, have an anti-Jewish bias—that they deny opportunities to Jewish doctors and nurses? It seems to us that even before the public was given the figures that out of 130 physicians and surgeons, 120 are Jewish, they should have realized how absurd this false charge is.

CLAIM THAT HOSPITAL IS RUN BY A GROUP OF BUSINESS MEN

This critic also makes the charge that a group of business men run the hospital in a purely commercial way, guided neither by medical personnel, nor by trained hospital personnel, with the result that the expenses of this hospital are considerably higher than those of any other hospital.

If the Montefiore Hospital were run completely by a group of business men, in a purely commercial way, it would be reasonable to suppose that it would be run more economically than any other hospital and that, therefore, our expenses would be lower instead of higher than in any other institution. The fact of the matter is that the hospital has not been so run; the Medical Board of the hospital actually and effectively functions in all medical matters. The Medical Board of the hospital consists of every Chief of the hospital—27 in number. This Board in turn appoints its own committees to function in their several specific departments. There is, for instance, a Laboratory Committee, an Interne Committee, a Committee on Operating Room Technique, a School of Nursing Committee, an Out Patient Department Committ, a Scientific Program Committee, a Committee on Medical Records, and the Conference Committee, which as a part of the Joint Conference Committee, functions jointly with the Committee on Medical Affairs, which the Board of Trustees appoints and approves.

CLAIM THAT MONTEFIORE HOSPITAL CHARGES TO PATIENTS ARE GREATER THAN THOSE OF OTHER HOSPITALS

The standard ward rate for hospitals in this city, including Montefiore, is $3.00 per day—this in spite of the fact that our largest ward consists of only four beds, while wards in other hospitals, for which the same $3.00 rate is charged, have as high as five to ten times that number of beds. The semi-private rate for hospitals, including Montefiore, is $4.00 a day. While private rooms in other hospitals range from $5.00 to $15.00 per day, in Montefiore Hospital the range is from $5.00 to only $12.00.

CLAIM THAT MONTEFIORE HOSPITAL IS DOING LESS FREE WORK THAN ANY OTHER INSTITUTION IN THE CITY

As a matter of statistical record here and in Harrisburg, the Montefiore Hospital does 16 per cent of all the free dispensary work done in the City of Pittsburgh. Of the eighteen hospitals within the city limits, each with its free dispensary, besides the Pittsburgh Free Dispensary, the Falk Clinic, and the Pittsburgh Skin and Cancer Foundation, Montefiore is doing far more than its share of the free work of the City of Pittsburgh. In addition, during the years of depression, nearly 50 per cent of our "house" or in-patient service has been on a totally free basis.

CHARGE OF INCORRECT KEEPING OF BOOKS

Another charge is to the effect that our "boast of finishing the year without a deficit is nothing more than the result of clever bookkeeping."

We have never made the statement that we have finished the year without a deficit. We have had, and will have for some time to come, an enormous deficit at the end of each year due our mortgage interest payments, which amount to $35,000 annually. What we have tried to show the public at our annual meeting is that, aside from this inescapable deficit, the actual operating expense of the hospital has been kept as closely as possible within its income. It is absurd for any one to think that these figures could be changed by clever bookkeeping, since our accounts are gone over quarterly by Bachrach, Sanderbeck & Co., certified public accounts, by representatives of the State Auditor-General, and by Auditors of the State Department of Public Welfare.

Here again we have an illustration of the utter worthlessness of the charges. Our critic does not seem to have the ability to understand its absurdity. Boiled down, the charge means this: that the amount which we expand is in excess of our receipts and that by "clever bookkeeping" we hide that fact. He fails to realize that if bills are contracted for expenses, the money to pay them must be gotten somewhere. There is no escape from that fact. No bookkeeping can be used as a substitute for money. If there were any truth in this absurd charge, it would have been easy for this man to have furnished definite, concrete information on the subject, showing how much the expense of operating the hospital was, if he claims the figures reported by the hospital are incorrect, and where he got this information. However, it is like the rest of his charges—mere general statements, accusations, without any FACTS to support them.

January 11, 1935   THE JEWISH CRITERION   *Five*

Association of Western Pennsylvania

The expenses of Montefiore Hospital, compared with other hospitals, show that its daily per capita costs—the cost of running the institution for a day, divided by the number of patients for that day—compare more than favorably with the daily per capita costs of hospitals of approximately the same size in this city and in other cities.

In comparing per capita costs, it must be remembered that the larger the hospital, the lower the daily per capita cost becomes. In other words, if one divides the expenses of running a hospital by a greater number of patients, the individual cost is necessarily lowered. The following comparative figures, therefore, are interesting:

Daily per capita cost of a Pittsburgh hospital of 400 beds..$5.09
Daily per capita cost of a hospital in a nearby city very
close in size to Montefiore.....................$6.63
Daily per capita cost of a New York hospital with 115 more
beds than Montefiore.......................$5.76
Daily per capita cost of another New York hospital of 75
more beds than Montefiore...................$6.36
Daily per capita cost of a New York hospital with 30 beds
less than Montefiore.........................$6.81

AS AGAINST

**DAILY PER CAPITA COST OF MONTE-
FIORE HOSPITAL** $5.23
—225 BEDS—

We present further the following striking figures for the year 1933, for comparison of income and expense of a hospital in another city, of about the same type as Montefiore, and approximately the same size:

	Montefiore Hospital 225 Beds	Out-of-Town Hospital 270 Beds
Total Income	$292,904.79	$371,271.00
Accounts Receivable 12/31/33..	26,338.28	75,314.00
Accounts and Notes Payable...	7,128.16	39,881.00
Salaries and Wages	168,434.13	255,785.90
Total Patient Days—In Patient	51,618	50,900
Free Days—In Patient	24,422	20,203

Standard of Montefiore's Practices and Methods

The charge is made that the hospital, being in the control of lay people only, some of the practices are not in accordance with standard hospital methods.

Franklin H. Martin, M. D., Director-General of the American College of Surgeons, writes under date of October 15, 1934: "We have pleasure in informing you that your hospital has been awarded full approval by the American College of Surgeons for the year 1934. Approval is given from year to year to the hospitals that comply fully with the requirements as laid down in the Minimum Standard of the American College of Surgeons."

These standards are made in the interest of the patients and are so recognized by our sister hospitals and their medical and surgical staffs.

The Montefiore Hospital is unqualifiedly approved for internships by the Council on Medical Education and Hospitals of the American Medical Association, and by the State Board of Medical Education and Licensure.

KOSHER KITCHEN

Although less than 10 per cent of our patients desire this service, we nevertheless maintain in scrupulous detail strictly kosher kitchens, handled by a Jewish cook thoroughly familiar with kosher ritual and who is in her own home a strict observer of kashruth.

OUR DIRECTOR

Attacks have been made upon our Director on the grounds that such a position should be held only by a doctor, and alleging therefore his general unfitness for the position.

The Hospital Conference of Pittsburgh includes in its membership the directing heads of forty-two hospitals in Western Pennsylvania. Of these hospitals, only one has as its managing head a doctor. Our Director has been engaged in hospital work during the past five years and is a member of this organization, which last year elected him its president.

Surely the group of men who are responsible for the direct management of the hospitals of Pittsburgh should be well qualified to judge of the fitness and ability of any man engaged in similar work, and their approval of his standing as a hospital executive by according him this signal honor, should be a conclusive answer to the opinion of his self-appointed critics. His achievements not only at Montefiore but in the community at large and in the general field of hospital activity speak for themselves.

Against destructive criticism, we present five years of development and growth in the Montefiore Hospital. In the administration of the hospital, we have accepted as a basic principle of proper hospital organization and function, the theory that the hospital is the health center of the community which it serves; that it is our province to supply every known means for the diagnosis and treatment of disease properly supplemented with adequate equipment, a n d personnel specially trained; that it is our province, too, to go beyond this and promote through example set within the hospital and through its service, a higher standard of health care, acting as a preventative health force throughout the community. We have been motivated by the thought that the hospital is not only an institution for healing and direct service to the patient, but is an institution as well, which carries a responsibility in the field of teaching.

We have had in our minds, in other words, the thought that the function of the hospital of today is four-fold. First of all, it is an institution of service to the patient; secondly, it is a teaching center for the interne and the younger doctor, for training student nurses, dietitians, technicians for the various laboratories, and administrative personnel. Thirdly, it is a center for research in the study of disease—for the discovery of the treatment and cure of diseases which still baffle the medical practitioner of today; for the improvement of methods of treatment already known. Fourthly, the hospital is a promotional agency in the field of preventative medicine.

We have been building an institution worthy of the name it carries and worthy of the community it represents.

**THE MONTEFIORE HOSPITAL
ASSOCIATION OF WESTERN
PENNSYLVANIA**

Liliane S. Kaufmann,
PRESIDENT

SOURCES:

"Statement of the Montefiore Hospital Association of Western Pennsylvania," by Liliane S. Kaufmann, *Jewish Criterion*, January 11, 1935, p. 4-5

"Critics Have Opportunity to Voice Grievances at Montefiore Annual Meeting," *Jewish Criterion*, January 25, 1935, p. 5

"Modern Gothic," by Kevin Gray, *New York Times*, September 23, 2001

Kaufmann's Department Store Records, 1868-2003, MSS 371, Rauh Jewish Archives, Thomas and Katherine Detre Library and Archives, Senator John Heinz History Center

"Fallingwater, Rising: Frank Lloyd Wright, E. J. Kaufmann and America's most extraordinary house," by Franklin Toker, A.A. Knopf, 2003

Montefiore Hospital, Records, 1899-1998, MSS 286, Rauh Jewish Archives, Thomas and Katherine Detre Library and Archives, Senator John Heinz History Center

Elaine Lobl Konigsburg

(February 10, 1930–April 19, 2013)

by Ruth C. Reidbord

What makes a person a legend? Perhaps a significant role in science, government, the arts. A person who makes a difference. Someone who will be remembered after she dies. But by whom?

Elaine Lobl Konigsburg, known professionally as E.L. Konigsburg, was such a person. Her name may not be on the lips of the general public. Yet ask many young people and many who would be considered "baby boomers" who she is, and they will tell you about the books they cherished that she wrote. Or maybe they won't remember her name. But they'll remember *The Mixed Up Files of Mrs. Basil E. Frankweiler; Jennifer, Hecate, Macbeth, William McKinley, and Me, Elizabeth;* or *Father's Arcane Daughter.* Fewer will know that Konigsburg grew up in Western Pennsylvania, went to college in Pittsburgh and maintained strong ties in Pittsburgh for the rest of her life. Some will know that she was Jewish, although those roots weren't immediately apparent.

Today, when many young people struggle to get a college education and carve out a life consistent with their aspirations, E.L. Konigsburg surely deserves notice. She struggled to learn, to read and to afford higher education and ultimately became one of only six authors to win two Newbery Medals, the highest honor in children's literature. How did she do it?

Konigsburg was born February 10, 1930 in New York to Adolph and Beulah Klein Lobl, working class parents of Hungarian Jewish heritage. The family lived in several towns in Western Pennsylvania and Ohio when Konigsburg was quite young and ultimately moved to Farrell, Pa., where her father owned a bar. The parents worked hard to feed and clothe their three daughters. Elaine, as the middle daughter, made do with clothes sewn by her mother. No one in the family seemed to care about anything outside of day-to-day living, so Elaine found, quite early, that if she wanted to read—and she did—she would have to do it in the one bathroom in their apartment, lit by a bare light bulb. There she would hide at night and read books like *The Secret Garden* and *Mary Poppins*. If a particularly sad passage moved her to tears, she would flush the toilet to keep her parents from hearing her crying.

Although she was valedictorian at Farrell High School and editor of the school newspaper, she had no guidance counselors to help her figure what to do about college and no money to pay for tuition. She decided to apply to the chemistry program at the Margaret Morrison Carnegie College

for Women at the Carnegie Institute of Technology (now
Carnegie Mellon University). She worked as a bookkeeper at
the Shenango Valley Provision Company meat plant for a
year after graduating from high school. There, she met her
future husband, David Konigsburg, a relative of the owner.

In her freshman year at Carnegie Tech, Elaine took a required
English Composition course taught by a new instructor, Dr. A.
Fred Sochatoff, a short man with a huge heart hidden behind a
rather formal style. This class and this man were to play a significant part in Konigsburg's life. In the spring of her freshman year,
Konigsburg was walking on "The Cut," a grassy walkway down
the center of the Carnegie Tech campus, when she encountered
her teacher. "Miss Lobl," Sochatoff said, "what are your plans
for the summer and what courses have you selected to take for
your sophomore year?" Konigsburg, who had not confided in
anyone at Carnegie Tech about her financial straits, said she
would have to drop out and work for a year to earn money
for her second year of college. To which Dr. Sochatoff replied,
"Miss Lobl, a student of your ilk cannot be allowed to drop out.
Let me see what I can do." He turned to his wife, Belle Binstock
Sochatoff, who was a sister-in-law of Mrs. Dorothy Binstock,
a well-known community leader in Pittsburgh. Together
they were instrumental in securing financial aid for Elaine's
sophomore year. She supplemented the scholarship funds by
managing a dormitory laundry and working as a playground
instructor, a waitress and a library page.

With this help she was able to finish her college education, graduating with honors in 1952. The die had been cast.
As Dr. A. Fred Sochatoff's youngest daughter Dr. Mildred
Sochatoff Myers remembers, Konigsburg became part of
the Sochatoff family. These strong bonds continued after

Dr. Sochatoff died in 1987, through the efforts of his daughters. Mildred was in touch with Konigsburg until Konigsburg died in 2013. Fittingly, Konigsburg expressed her relationship with Dr. Sochatoff better than anyone. When she received a Distinguished Alumna Award from Carnegie Mellon University in 1999 she said, "The only course in writing I have ever had was Freshman Composition, taught by Dr. A. Fred Sochatoff. One of my books is dedicated to him. It says: *For Fred Sochatoff – who was there at the beginning, before either of us knew it was a beginning.* Dr. Sochatoff and I had both arrived here when the school was under the Carnegie Plan. We students were to be taught how to solve problems. In Freshman Composition that translated into being taught how to explain or describe difficult processes or concepts in a straightforward manner. And in our literature course, we were taught how to interpret the bells and whistles but not write with them. To this day, I cannot think of any better training for any writer."

Today, the young girl who read by the light of the exposed bulb in her bathroom is recognized as one of the finest storytellers of her genre. She twice received the Newbery Medal, the highest honor in children's literature, and had the rare honor of being a winner and a runner-up in the same year—and for her first two published books.

In July 1952, after graduating, Elaine married David Konigsburg, who was by then an industrial psychologist. They would have three children together—Paul, Laurie and Ross. As a graduate student at the University of Pittsburgh from 1952 to 1954, Elaine Konigsburg worked as a research assistant in a tissue culture laboratory. She taught science at Bartram, a private girls' school in Jacksonville, Florida in 1954, and again

In addition to her writing, E. L. Konigsburg was an illustrator and regularly sketched scenes from her novels. This drawing depicts the titular team of her 1969 baseball novel *About the B'nai Bagels*. (document courtesy of Elaine Lobl Konigsburg Papers, 1967-1986, SC.1986.01, Special Collections Department, University of Pittsburgh)

from 1960 to 1962, after a break to raise her children. When her husband was transferred to New York in 1962, and her children were enrolled in school, she began to write. The inspiration for her first novel came from watching her daughter Laurie hesitantly discover new friends after moving to Port Chester, N.Y., an experience which culminated in *Jennifer, Hecate, Macbeth, William McKinley, and Me, Elizabeth* (1967). In the late 1960s, then a Jacksonville housewife with no agent, Konigsburg mailed this story of friendship and witchcraft to Atheneum Books in New York. While waiting for its publication, she began *From the Mixed-up Files of Mrs. Basil E. Frankweiler.*

E. L. Konigsburg wrote her first novel, *Jennifer, Hecate, Macbeth, William McKinley, and Me, Elizabeth,* while raising her children in New York and Florida during the 1960s. These three drafts of the first page of the 1967 novel provide insight into her revision process. (document courtesy of Elaine Lobl Konigsburg Papers, 1967-1986, SC.1986.01, Special Collections Department, University of Pittsburgh)

Konigsburg's books are full of old women, the most famous being Mrs. Basil E. Frankweiler of the Newbery Award-winning *From the Mixed-Up Files of Mrs. Basil E. Frankweiler.* Frankweiler frames and narrates the story of Claudia and Jamie Kincaid, a sister and brother who run away from their home in a Connecticut suburb and live in the Metropolitan Museum of Art. Toward the end of the novel, Claudia and

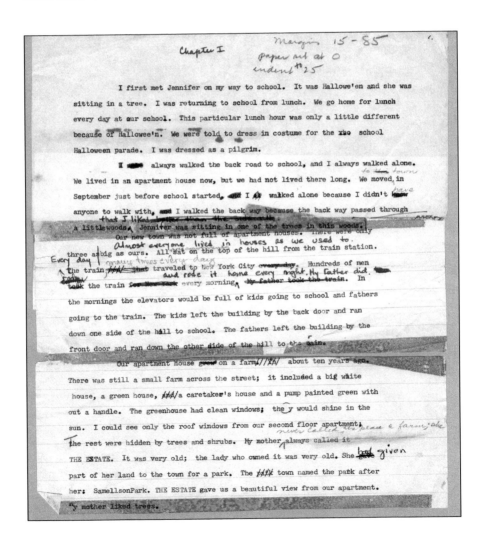

12/15 Baskerville x 22 pieces

1st 3 lines of type to be indented 5 ems (am sorry to put in a spat: ellus) Jennifer, "Heirati", it

later which is to re ase mo, pp 1-76

for all chap pp

Chapter I

————I first met Jennifer on my way to school. It was Hallowe'en, and she was sitting in a tree. I was ~~returning~~ to school from lunch. ~~We go home for lunch every day at our school.~~ This particular lunch hour was only a little different, because of Hallowe'en. We were told to dress in costume for the school Hallowe'en parade. I was dressed as a Pilgrim.

I always walked the back road to school, and I always walked alone. ~~We lived in an apartment house now, but we had not lived there long.~~ We moved to, town in September just before school started, I walked alone because I didn't have anyone to walk with. I walked the back way because ~~the back way~~ it passed through a little woods that I liked. Jennifer was sitting in one of the trees in this woods.

Our apartment house had grown on a farm about ten years ago. There was still a small farm across the street; it included a big white house, a green house, a caretaker's house, and a pump painted green without a handle. The greenhouse had clean windows; they ~~would shine~~ shone in the sun. I could see only the roof windows from our second floor apartment. The rest were hidden by trees and shrubs. My mother never called the place a farm; she always called it THE ESTATE. It was ~~very~~ old; the lady who owned it was ~~very~~ old. She had given part of her land to the town for a park, and the town named the park after her: Samellson Park. THE ESTATE gave us a beautiful view from our apartment. My mother liked trees.

Our new town was not full of apartment ~~houses~~. Almost everyone else lived in houses, ~~as we used to~~. There were only three apartment buildings as big as ours. All three sat on the top of the hill from the

Jamie wind up at the house of the wealthy and reclusive Frankweiler. She is no one's grandmother, and she doesn't soften herself for her young visitors; her tone is dry and she speaks to them directly, without condescension, and cuts them a deal. As in all of Konigsburg's books, the children and the adults take each other very seriously. As one of her characters puts it, "Kids are amateur adults." According to Dr. Millie Sochatoff Myers, this inclination to treat young people of merit as adults was something that Millie experienced as a teenager invited to tea at Elaine's home in Pittsburgh shortly after she was married. Elaine treated Millie "as the adult I so much wanted to be."

Some people have wondered whether being Jewish influenced Konigsburg's writing. A few of her characters are explicitly Jewish. Many are outsiders who can't stop thinking about being different. Konigsburg's books are about these characters finding and recognizing one another without really talking about it, recognizing one another not as victims but as fellow travelers and figuring out how to live in a world that doesn't always see them.

Some might also wonder whether her scientific education and subsequent teaching experience influenced her writing. Writing about Konigsburg in the Library of Author Biographies series, author Renee Ambrosek posits a theory that Konigsburg used the scientific method throughout her career, even though she probably wasn't conscious of following the scientific method as her career developed. According to Ambrosek, Konigsburg approached problems like a scientist. She concludes, "Certainly in the case of E.L. Konigsburg, necessity has been the mother of invention time and time again."

She had a special interest in middle-class children and their adolescence—"the problems," she said, "that come about even though you don't have to worry if you wear out your shoes." She said she strove to write literature "that tackles the basic problems of who am I? What makes me the same as everyone else? What makes me different?" Once one knows that Konigsburg grew up in impoverished circumstances, it is remarkable that she chose to focus on middle class children. She wrote about children who had a completely different background, but she saw the commonality in their experiences.

Throughout the years, although she lived primarily in Jacksonville, Konigsburg maintained her connections in Pittsburgh. Dr. Millie Sochatoff Myers noted these connections in a letter to the editor of the *Pittsburgh Post-Gazette* in 2013, after Konigsburg died: "Elaine returned to Pittsburgh many times, speaking at children's book festivals and conferences at Carnegie Library and at the University of Pittsburgh. The Elaine Lobl Konigsburg Papers reside in the Elizabeth Nesbitt Room at Pitt's School of Library and Information Sciences. In 2001, a Japanese scholar who was translating her works into Japanese came to Pittsburgh to use that archive. Elaine was to meet her here, but her husband's death canceled that trip. At Elaine's request, I greeted the Japanese visitors and gave them the tour of Carnegie Mellon that Elaine had promised them, because they wanted to see where her career began.

"(One of her) books, 'Father's Arcane Daughter,' is set in Pittsburgh and refers to 'the house on North Negley Avenue.' That was my family's house."

Konigsburg died following a stroke on April 19, 2013. One of the people who spoke at her funeral was Joseph Ellovich, who was not only her dear friend from Sharon, a town near Farrell, but remained close to her and her family for the rest of her life. He saw first hand, at an early age, the bright mind, the inquisitive and observant spirit, the enormous determination to succeed that would serve her well throughout her life. His sister Marcia Ellovich Frumerman also remained in touch with Elaine through the years and attended most of the literary events at which she spoke in Pittsburgh as well as the Carnegie Mellon Commencement exercises in 1999 when Konigsburg received the Alumna award.

This literary legend began her life in the Pittsburgh area, found her first inspiration here at Carnegie Mellon and continued her association with Pittsburgh throughout her life.

SOURCES:

"E. L. Konigsburg, Author, Is Dead at 83," by Paul Vitello, *New York Times*, April 22, 2013

"E.L. Konigsburg, author of 'From the Mixed-up Files of Mrs. Basil E. Frankweiler' and other children's classics, dies at 83," by Emily Langer, *Washington Post*, April 22, 2013

Jewish Women's International, 2013

"Remembering E.L. Konigsburg," by Abigail Miller, Tablet Magazine (online), April 23, 2013

The Library of Author Biographies 2006

"The Author E.L. Konigsburg had many ties to Pittsburgh," letter to the editor by Dr. Mildred Sochatoff Myers, *Pittsburgh Post-Gazette*, May 1, 2013

Telephone interviews with Joseph Ellovich who lives in Burlington, Vermont, and Dr. Mildred (Millie) Sochatoff Myers, professor in the Tepper School of Business at Carnegie Mellon University

Personal discussions with Marcia Ellovich Frumerman.

Sophie Masloff
(December 23, 1917–August 17, 2014)

by Laura Cherner

S ophie Masloff was the first female mayor of Pittsburgh and the first Jewish mayor of the city in more than 150 years. Her rise to power was a combination of ambition and chance. Similarly, her time in office was marked by her response to dramatic changes in the city and by her endearing nature.

Sophie Friedman was the youngest of four children born to Romanian immigrants in the Hill District. Her father Louis Friedman died soon after the family arrived in the United States. Her mother Jennie Friedman, who spoke only Yiddish and Romanian, supported the family by rolling stogies. "It was a typical Orthodox Jewish family. My mother was steeped

(photograph courtesy of Sophie Masloff Papers, 1977-1992, MSS#589, Rauh Jewish Archives, Thomas and Katherine Detre Library and Archives, Senator John Heinz History Center)

in tradition, steeped in superstition and extremely devout," Masloff said in a 1987 oral history with the National Council of Jewish Women, Pittsburgh Section. Financial demands during the Great Depression forced Masloff to decline a scholarship to the University of Pittsburgh and instead enter the workforce immediately after graduating from Fifth Avenue High School in 1935. She later claimed — with pride — to have worked every single day from her high school graduation until her mayoral appointment.

Building on acquaintances she had made campaigning for the Democratic Party as a student, she got a job in the county tax office in 1936. She had to lie about her age to qualify for a job. While working for the county, she started dating Jack Masloff, who had previously flirted with her when she would pass his house on Dinwiddie Street on the way to Fifth Avenue High School. They eloped in 1939 and kept their marriage a secret to sidestep Depression-era employment policies that forbade spouses from both working for county government. They were married for 52 years and had one daughter, Linda.

When a vacancy emerged, Masloff moved into the office of County Commissioner John Kane. She later took a job in the assignment room of the Allegheny County Court of Common Pleas, where she stayed for more than 30 years. During her decades as a government employee, she nurtured her interest in politics. She joined Democratic Party organizations, served on boards and attended conventions, all while raising her daughter and seeing to household responsibilities more commonly associated with traditional homemakers. These efforts brought her historic distinctions. She was the first Jewish president of the Pennsylvania Federation of Democratic Women and was secretary of the Democratic

Sophie Masloff taking the oath of office as mayor of Pittsburgh on January 2, 1990. As city council president, Masloff was automatically appointed mayor when her predecessor Richard S. Caliguiri died in office in 1988. She was elected to a full-term in office and was the first woman to hold the position. (photograph courtesy of Sophie Masloff Papers, 1977-1992, MSS#589, Rauh Jewish Archives, Thomas and Katherine Detre Library and Archives, Senator John Heinz History Center)

Women's Guild of Allegheny County. Her associations within the Democratic Party helped her win a special election in 1976 to fill a vacancy on City Council. She retained the seat in regular elections in 1977, 1981 and 1985. She advocated for various issues but was most pleased with practical accomplishments such as bringing cable television to the city and expanding amenities for senior citizens. She also participated in Jewish communal institutions, such as Hadassah and B'nai B'rith. Her advocacy for Soviet Jewry included a courageous trip to the former Soviet Union.

Her rise to the mayoral office was providential. She became the first female president of City Council in 1988 after her predecessor resigned in a corruption scandal and her competitors lost their council seats. She had only been in the position for five months when Mayor Richard S. Caliguiri died of amyloidosis

In this early profile in *The Jewish Chronicle,* Sophie Masloff described her difficult upbringing in the Hill District and her apprenticeship in Pittsburgh politics. (document courtesy of the Pittsburgh Jewish Newspaper Project)

and she was appointed to finish his term. The following year, she ran unopposed and won a full term in office.

Masloff welcomed her reputation as an "old Jewish grandmother" while continuing the hardnosed urban revitalization campaign Caliguiri had launched with his Renaissance II initiative. Her administration advanced three major real estate developments: Crawford Square, Washington's Landing and the Pittsburgh Technology Center. Responding to financial shortfalls after the collapse of the steel industry, she privatized costly city-owned properties such as the Pittsburgh Zoo and Phipps Conservatory and helped create the Regional Asset District to fund cultural organizations in the city. She twice cut the city wage tax. She threatened to close city bank accounts unless area financial institutions addressed the impact of redlining on minority communities. She intervened in a 28-day transit strike in 1992, worried about its impact on those who depended on bus service to get to work and to the doctor. She helped launch the first "blue-bag" recycling program in the city, which remains in effect.

Masloff was notorious for her gaffes and malapropisms. She called musicians The Who "The How" and Bruce Springsteen "Bruce Bedspring." When presidential candidate Bill Clinton called her, in 1992, she thought it was a prank and famously responded, "Yeah, and this is the Queen of Sheba." Although the media often lampooned Masloff for these incidents, she insisted they reflected her good humor. "In some situations, where you have to listen to a lot of boring speeches, I can't resist the opportunity to say something silly. But some people are not too humorous, and lately, I've come to the place where I limit joking around because it might look like I don't know any better," she said in a 1992 interview. Her personality won her popular appeal but occasionally created obstacles. She was fiercely ridiculed in 1991 for proposing Clemente Field, a charming riverfront baseball stadium. The idea became a reality in 2001 with the construction of PNC Park, which is widely considered one of the greatest stadiums in professional sports.

Even after her time as mayor ended in 1993, Masloff remained popular in her hometown. She continued serving on government boards and running for low-level political offices. Between 1973 and 2000, she won fifteen straight elections, according to her longtime adviser John Seidman. In honor of her 90th birthday, and to acknowledge her work towards making PNC Park a reality, the city named a street near the stadium Sophie Masloff Way. She prided herself on being relatable. She was regularly greeted with "Hi Sophie" while running errands or performing her duties as mayor. By modernizing the stereotype of "old Jewish grandmother," Masloff won her way into the hearts of citizens and made an indelible mark on the city of Pittsburgh at a crucial time.

SOURCES:

Masloff, Sophie, oral history interview, 1987, *Pittsburgh and Beyond: the Experience of the Jewish Community,* National Council of Jewish Women, Pittsburgh Section, Oral History Collection at the University of Pittsburgh (http://images.library.pitt.edu/cgi-bin/i/image/image-idx?view=entry;cc=ncjw;entryid=x-ais196440.299)

Masloff, Sophie, oral history interview, 1994, *Pittsburgh and Beyond: the Experience of the Jewish Community,* National Council of Jewish Women, Pittsburgh Section, Oral History Collection at the University of Pittsburgh (http://images.library.pitt.edu/cgi-bin/i/image/image-idx?view=entry;cc=ncjw;entryid=x-ais196440.511)

Sophie Masloff Papers, 1977-1992, MSS#589, Rauh Jewish Archives, Thomas and Katherine Detre Library and Archives, Senator John Heinz History Center

"Former mayor Sophie Masloff remembered as 'the embodiment of our city,'" by Jon Schmitz, *Pittsburgh Post-Gazette,* August 18, 2014 (http://www.post-gazette.com/local/city/2014/08/18/folksy-masloff-made-history-as-city-s-first-woman-mayor/201408170206, accessed November 25, 2015)

"The Councilman is a Lady!" by Albert W. Bloom, *Jewish Chronicle,* March 10, 1977, p. 8

"Pittsburgh Mayor Seeks New Image: From Grandmother to Tough Leader," by Michael deCourcy Hinds, *New York Times,* January 22, 1992

Bernice Goldman Preisser

(March 18, 1917–July 28, 1994)

by Jane C. Arkus

S he was a woman in what was called "a man's game," a pio-
neer among marketing professionals, a force for positive
change in her community, a mentor revered by future marketing leaders — in short, a lead player in business and community
at a time when women were rarely welcome in the corporate
boardroom (except to serve the coffee).

Bernice Goldman Preisser was born in Pittsburgh in 1917,
the third child of Ethyl and "Second Story Morry," a legendary retailer who, in the midst of the Great Depression, ran
a bustling menswear business in downtown Pittsburgh, one
flight up from the sidewalk. This not only saved him money
on rent but lent itself to colorful promotions. ("Climb up one

(photograph courtesy of Jane Arkus)

flight, save $15.") Morry Goldman used marketing practices that were innovative for the '20s and '30s, and it is often assumed that Bernice inherited her advertising and merchandising genes from her father.

After majoring in English at the Universities of Pittsburgh and Wisconsin, like so many young job seekers of fame and fortune in the big city, she took a fling at New York. Her intent: to study voice and aim at a career in opera. As a source of income she landed a secretarial job at a small advertising agency, and while there, discovered she had an aptitude for copy writing. Gone were the voice lessons. With characteristic objectivity, she recognized that she was not to be a diva at the Met, (but she did do some very funny imitations). Humor — never taking herself too seriously — was one of the traits that graced her teaching and endeared her over the years to those she taught and those she served. With World War II sending lives into upheaval, Bernice headed back to Pittsburgh where she entered her first "real" job. She took up the reins at another small agency founded by her older brother, while he served in the U.S. Navy. This meant doing a bit of everything: information gathering, time-and-space-buying, ad writing, jingle producing and client hand-holding until her big brother came home.

All these experiences were priming her for her next big leap — to Los Angeles and a career that, from then on, spiraled upward. She was tapped by the May Company department store as TV director, virtually inventing the first job of its kind in the country. (For two years, she produced a daytime show emceed by Betty White). She went on to the Broadway stores as special events director and later joined Wade Advertising as senior writer on the Alka-Seltzer account, part of the team

Bernice Preisser was a leader in the marketing communications world at a time when few women advanced to leadership positions. She started her career at a small agency in Pittsburgh before moving to Los Angeles where she worked in radio and the new medium — television. By the time she returned to Pittsburgh in 1954, she had honed her skills in the targeted use of broadcast and print media and was much in demand among agencies. (photograph courtesy of Jane Arkus)

that invented Speedy Alka Seltzer and its famous jingle, "Plop, plop, fizz, fizz, oh what a relief it is."

Throughout her career it was Bernice's unique understanding of the consumer mind and consumer markets that lifted her above the pack. After her divorce from a Hollywood screenwriter, single again and with a young son, she opted in 1954 to continue her career back in Pittsburgh, where loving grandparents would care for Ted at the end of the school day.

As head of consumer and business-to-business marketing at Lando Inc., Bernice oversaw promotional projects for some of the most prestigious advertisers in the region, including U.S. Steel. Shown here is a promotional mailer directed at businesses in search of space and a part of a campaign to promote the environmental and economic advantages of the steel can to the packaging trade. (documents courtesy Jane Arkus)

Join The Great Space Adventure.
The U.S. Steel Building in Pittsburgh.

Come soar sky-high with us at the top of Pittsburgh's
Golden Triangle. Home of 50 great U.S.
corporations, commercial and professional firms.
Known for its spectacular view, flexible spaces, built-
in luxuries, enviable location. Economical, too.
For information, phone or write
H. Ross Ford, Jr., John W. Galbreath & Co. Realtors,
U.S. Steel Building, Pittsburgh PA 15219.
(412) 391-8950.

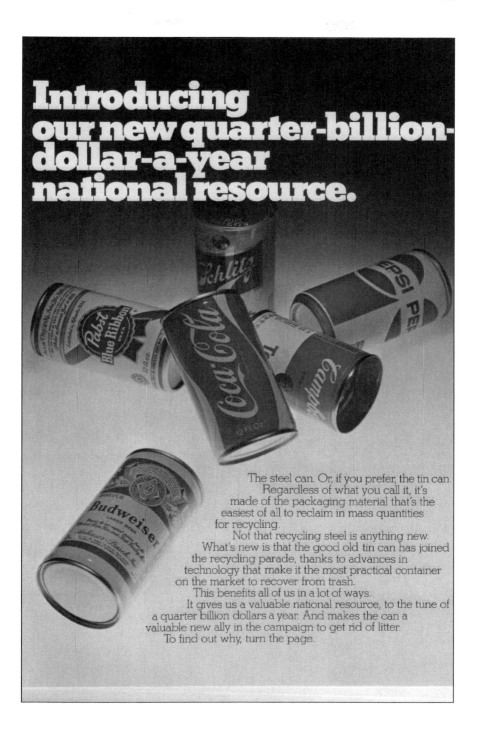

Introducing our new quarter-billion-dollar-a-year national resource.

The steel can. Or, if you prefer, the tin can. Regardless of what you call it, it's made of the packaging material that's the easiest of all to reclaim in mass quantities for recycling.

Not that recycling steel is anything new. What's new is that the good old tin can has joined the recycling parade, thanks to advances in technology that make it the most practical container on the market to recover from trash.

This benefits all of us in a lot of ways.

It gives us a valuable national resource, to the tune of a quarter billion dollars a year. And makes the can a valuable new ally in the campaign to get rid of litter.

To find out why, turn the page.

Her reputation had preceded her, and she was snapped up quickly by Lando Inc., a fast-growing entrepreneurial ad agency where she was made assistant to the president. Lured away by Ketchum, McLeod and Grove, Pittsburgh's largest agency, she broke new barriers, becoming Ketchum's first woman account executive, and later, department head, vice-president of strategic planning. Returning to Lando (now merged with the international ad agency Marsteller Advertising) she was made partner, and on her retirement in the early 1990s formed a consultancy with a close friend and longtime advertising associate, Jane C. Arkus.

Long before "consumerism" became a household word she was a champion of the consumer's right to intelligent, informative advertising. During her career spanning more than 40 years, she put her strategic mind, wisdom and creativity to work for national and regional consumer and business-to-business clients, among them The Athlete's Foot shoe stores, Foodland supermarkets, Westinghouse appliances, PPG fiberglass draperies, Isaly's Chipped Chopped Ham and U.S. Steel recyclable cans. She received countless awards for her work, including some of the most prestigious in the field.

At the same time she was also a force in community affairs, donating her time and skills pro bono to a wide variety of human-service, cultural and educational non-profits. She conducted classes at the University of Pittsburgh, Carnegie Mellon University, Duquesne University, the University of Michigan and Chatham College (now Chatham University); served as president of Job Advisory Services; served on the boards of Civic Light Opera and Vocational Rehabilitation Center; and helped position and promote a substantial number of Jewish institutions including Riverview senior care center,

Jewish Residential Services, the National Council of Jewish Women, the Ladies Hospital Aid Society, Horizon Homes Inc., Montefiore Hospital, and Rodef Shalom Congregation.

Above all, it has been said among those in her wide orbit that Bernice Preisser invented the word "mentor." Among her other gifts she had a knack for helping businesses and people grow to the extent of their potential. It was her essential humanity and generosity of spirit that led her always to have time, an open door, and valuable words for those who sought guidance. Perhaps her greatest legacy lies in the number of Bernice's "graduates," who became the next generation of marketing leaders in the Pittsburgh region and beyond.

SOURCES:

"Maurice Goldman dies, founder of clothing store," by Vince Leonard, *Pittsburgh Post-Gazette,* June 24, 1983, p. 19

Morry and Ethel, by Stanley E. Goldman, S. Orleans, Mass., self-published, 1986

"Bernice G. Preisser, created winning U.S., local ad campaigns," by Dennis B. Roddy, *Pittsburgh Post-Gazette*, July 29, 1994, p. B-7

"Preisser ends 45-year ad career," by Edwin F. Brennan, *Pittsburgh Post-Gazette*, July 24, 1985, p. 29

"First Woman President for Advertising Club," by Jane Shaw, *Pittsburgh Post-Gazette*, September 15, 1975, p. 11

"Plenty of room in the hall of fame," by Christina Rouvalis, *Pittsburgh Post-Gazette,* August 10, 1997, p. C-5

"Innovative ad exec Preisser dead at 77," *Jewish Chronicle*, August 4, 1994, p. 38

"Make Bernice Proud," by Audrey Reichbaum, *Pittsburgh Post-Gazette*, September 10, 1994, p. D-3

Bertha Floersheim Rauh

(June 16, 1865–October 21, 1952)

by Corrine Azen Krause

Bertha Floersheim Rauh was born in Pittsburgh, Pa. on June 16, 1865, the daughter of Samuel and Pauline Wertheimer Floersheim, immigrants from western Germany. Dedicating her life to ameliorating the condition of the poor, the oppressed and the sick, she first worked for over twenty years as a volunteer and for a further twelve years as Director of the Department of Public Welfare of the City of Pittsburgh. She began her community service as a teenager, participating in aid to the Jewish immigrants from Eastern Europe. In 1888 she married Enoch Rauh (1857-1919), who was born in Dubuque, Iowa. Enoch's efforts to reform local politics earned him a fine

(photograph courtesy of Richard E. Rauh Papers, 1863-2012, MSS#301, Rauh Jewish Archives, Thomas and Katherine Detre Library and Archives, Senator John Heinz History Center)

reputation and a seat on the Pittsburgh City Council. Both the Rauh and Floersheim families were respected members of Rodef Shalom Temple, the Reform Jewish congregation of the city.

In 1904 Bertha Rauh was elected President of the National Council of Jewish Women, Pittsburgh Section, a position she held until 1919. In this respected volunteer post, she lectured and wrote, spreading the message that it was the responsibility of women to use their "leisure" time to extend mothering beyond their own children to the needy in the community. Rauh initiated several programs that were deemed necessary for public welfare and in consequence were taken over by the city. This was true of the Penny Lunches in public schools, social work at Juvenile Court, outdoor schools for tubercular children, a labor bureau to find jobs for the unemployed, and a Committee to Aid the Blind. This last committee soon formed the Western Pennsylvania Federation of the Blind, and later the National Association for the Blind.

Rauh was a founder of the Soho Public Baths, Consumers' League, Juvenile Court, and the "Pittsburgh and Allegheny Milk and Ice Association," which guaranteed pasteurized milk and pure water to poor children in the city. With the cooperation of the National Council of Jewish Women, Rauh argued successfully for penal reform and local and state laws regulating fund raising.

Interpreting commitment to suffrage in terms of expressing "compassion and caring" for women, children and the labor force through legislation, Rauh became a founding member of the Equal Franchise Society and of the Equal Franchise Federation of Western Pennsylvania. She distinguished between the contribution that women and men respectively could make, believing that women would bring sensitivity to decision-making positions, private charity, the city, and the nation. In a speech that was printed in full in the widely read *Jewish Criterion*, she criticized the Federation of Jewish Philanthropies for "a glaring error...the barring of women from the directorate." All the qualities that women would bring, Rauh continued, "constitute a unique contribution which deserves representation" in the work of all organizations, private or public, that make decisions affecting the people.

By 1919, Rauh was a member of thirty boards. In 1923 she was invited to serve on the Board of the Federation of Jewish Philanthropies for a one-year term until January, 1924.

Her experience in a wide range of civic projects and her proven executive ability made Bertha Rauh a highly qualified candidate for a responsible public position. In 1922, Bertha Rauh was the first woman appointed to a cabinet post, when Mayor William A. Magee invited her to serve as Director of Public Charities. His successors, Mayor Charles S. Kline and, later, John Herron, appointed her to two additional terms.

When Rauh assumed her position, a fellow cabinet member offered "congratulations and condolences," warning that it would take at least fifteen years "to set right the department." Bertha Rauh accomplished the challenging task in twelve years.

Her first significant move was to change the name of the department from "Public Charities" to the "Department of Public Welfare." In addition, she immediately launched a program of reform, developing a detailed plan for department improvements of which she sent drafts to political, social service and medical leaders before the work was begun. She collaborated closely with public and private charities,

settlement houses, hospitals, churches, and schools. She organized a committee of dietitians and other experienced food
service people to study the frequent food riots, and to recommend changes in diet. She convened a committee of nineteen
doctors to help plan improved medical facilities. By way of
organizing the work of the city office of the Department of
Public Welfare, Rauh established a Social Service Department,
a Mental Health Clinic, and a corps of District Physicians,
each to serve the sick poor in his or her district.

Rauh's greatest achievement was the transformation of the
overcrowded, understaffed, unsanitary and unsafe asylum
for the insane and indigent at the Mayview Hospital into a
modern psychiatric hospital. The Mayview City Home and
Hospital, located sixteen miles from the city of Pittsburgh,
consisted of a hospital, housing for the indigent and aging,
and a working farm. The physical facilities, from infrastruc-
ture to living and service areas, were in dire need of repair
and renovation. During her first year as Director of the
Department of Public Welfare, she introduced new clinics
and technologies at Mayview. Occupational therapy, physical therapy, hydro-therapy, oral, eye, nose and throat clinics,
a new Xray department, and new laboratories were added.
A genital-urinary clinic, the first in "an institution of this
kind," was begun.

Dr. Edward Mayer, a psychiatrist, headed a survey that
made recommendations for improvement. Plans were drawn
up from 1922 to 1927 when construction began. By 1932,
when the extensive renovations were almost completed, the
hospital was headed by a medical director and superintendent,
and staffed by ten physicians, seventeen visiting physicians,
two visiting psychiatrists, nurses and social workers. At that

time the population of Mayview numbered 3,000 people. Rauh also introduced a professional social worker to help discharged patients adjust to life outside the institution.

In 1924 and 1925 Rauh successfully lobbied the State Legislature to provide free burials for the indigent poor and "maintenance care and treatment" for the indigent insane. In response to reports of many cases of rabid dogs, Rauh asked the legislature to provide free Pasteur treatment for rabies victims and to require licensing and immunizing of dogs.

The Depression brought extraordinary demands on staff and facilities, forced the closing of the recently established Bureau for the Handicapped, and involved Rauh daily in referring applicants for relief. Associated Charities, Catholic Charities, Jewish Philanthropies, The Red Cross, U.S. Veterans Bureau, Salvation Army, Children's Aid Society, and Family and Children's Commission did their best to meet the requests and Rauh worked hard to secure help for all who qualified, keeping notes on each difficult case.

As her term came to a close Rauh was praised in articles and letters from many people. One executive commented that greater than all of the activities of her department "was the introduction of a sympathetic, understanding spirit of friendliness in the offices of the Department." The Director of Catholic Charities wrote, "Congratulations to you and City Council in passing the ordinance regulating the collection of money for charitable purposes. If you had done nothing else, you would have been a very successful Director of Public Welfare."

After her retirement from public office Rauh remained active in organization and civic life. She worked for the legalization of birth control and for smoke control. She advocated

Among her most notable achievements as Director of Public Welfare for the city
of Pittsburgh, Bertha Rauh overhauled the dysfunctional Mayview City Home and
Hospital into a modern psychiatric facility. She is seen here at a ribbon cutting for
a renovation of the center around 1928. (photograph courtesy of Richard E. Rauh
Papers, 1863-2012, MSS#301, Rauh Jewish Archives, Thomas and Katherine Detre
Library and Archives, Senator John Heinz History Center)

for a contagious disease hospital that would care for people
with sexually transmitted diseases, and urged moving the
General Hospital at Mayview into the city so that the sick
could receive regular high quality medical care.

Bertha Floersheim Rauh died on October 21, 1952. She was
survived by a son, Richard S. Rauh, a daughter, Helen Blanche
Rauh, and a grandson, Richard Enoch Rauh.

In a 1930 speech, Bertha Rauh recalled the early days of the Pittsburgh and Allegheny Milk and Ice Association, which provided pasteurized milk and clean water for poor children throughout the twin cities. (documents courtesy of Richard E. Rauh Papers, 1863-2012, MSS#301, Rauh Jewish Archives, Thomas and Katherine Detre Library and Archives, Senator John Heinz History Center)

– 1 –

One of the first public speeches I made, which stands out in my memory, was delivered before the Annual Meeting of the Pittsburgh and Allegheny Milk and Ice Association in October 1903.

This meeting was held in the old Chamber of Commerce Assembly Room in the Keenan Building and was largely attended by a group of prominent men and women interested in civic and philanthropic undertakings.

I well remember that added interest was given this meeting, as a new set of officers was proposed by the Nominating Committee, headed by the late Rt. Rev. Cortland Whitehead. The Bishop had visited me in my home and honored me by asking me to become President of the Association, which Presidency I have held for 27 years. I accepted the call and in making the address as the newly-elected Executive, I was exceedingly nervous. My knees trembled so, that throughout the delivery of this "speech" I was silently thanking the God who protects women, that long skirts were then the vogue and hid the shaking of those knees from the distinguished and discriminating audience!

Then upon gaining my mental equilibrium, I strove to impress upon my auditors that the work of the Association only was would be made possible through the cooperation of the public – through their enthusiasm, their encouragement, their support, and that only through these would the work go on in an effective and practicable manner.

I assured them that the fairies – the good fairies – were not all dead yet, even in those days of crass and rampant materialism, – that the real story of the founding of the work read like a fairy tale and like most fairy tales – ancient and modern – began with the story of a little child. I then recounted how a generous benefactor, Mr. W.S. Kuhn, had given a goodly sum to provide modified milk to save some sick infant, as his own child had been saved by modified milk; how he placed One Hundred ($100.) Dollars into the hands of Doctor Amelia Dranga, a member of the Board; and how she in looking about to minister to such a case, came face to face with the serious problem of sick and dying babies; that she at once associated herself with a few generous-hearted, broad-minded, public-spirited men and women, whic h action resulted in the formation of the Association.

To "Help Save The Babies" was the slogan of the organization. It was the inalienable right of every child I set forth, to be well born, to be reared healthfully and to be happy. Biologically, I said, the first two or three years of a child's life are extremely important, because these are the foundation years and for millions of children the whole of life is conditioned by these first few years.

The work I assured my hearers, was not only philanthropic but educational and patriotic as well, in that we would stimulate the public conscience into demanding a pure milk supply for the city and arouse an interest in the question. Given a pure whole milk during the first two years of its life we assure a child's physical. well-being; with this developed we may be sure to produce often a strong mentality; to strong mentality there must accrue a vigorous morality and a high sense of spirituality.

On every side, I declared, we hear the cry of the conservation of our natural resources. To my mind, I said, the conservation that should most seriously be looked into is the conservation of child life, for the child is the greatest asset of the state - it is the hope of the Nation.

I reminded my hearers that we are our brother's keeper and that it is for us to make ourselves permanently useful to those less fortunate babies. Why, I asked, will then our men and women, young and old, not aid in work such as this, for people suffer, (I insisted) and they grow sensibly lowered in vitality if they only pursue pleasure and freedom from care and responsibility. Those who remain away from work such as this, (I fairly shouted) lose the most, for there is nothing that so deadens the sympathies, nothing that so stunts the powers of enjoyment, as the constant keeping away

from the opportunities of helpfulness; and the persistent ignoring of the starvation struggles that make up half the race !. I sat down and Bishop Whitehead in his inimitable way - with a low bow to the audience and an equally chivalrous bow to me - said "Ladies and Gentlemen, we have chosen well; for aside the ability, the experience and the knowledge which Mrs. Rauh brings with her for our work, We have with us, a regular Chauncey Depewess." Hearty laughter greeted this finale. To this hour I can remember the painful embarrassment suffered through this couplet. I arose and with blood suffusing my face, I bowed in mock solemnity and retired precipitously in the audience.

[Editor's note: This profile originally appeared in "Jewish Women: A Comprehensive Historical Encyclopedia" and is republished with permission of the author.]

SOURCES:

MANUSCRIPTS:

Letter from "The Misses Shipley's School, Preparatory to Bryn Mawr College" to Bertha Rauh, September 18, 1907. The letter refused admission to Bertha Rauh's daughter, explaining, "It was easier, not only for us, but also for young girls who wished to be placed in a boarding school, that they should be in harmony with their surroundings. We have therefore been led to believe that the daughters of the Hebrew families can probably work better when placed with those of a similar line of thought." Archives of Industrial Society, University of Pittsburgh.

DeNardo, Diane C. " Bertha Floersheim Rauh: A Jewish volunteer social reformer forges a path to public office in Pittsburgh, Pennsylvania." Master's thesis, Duquesne University, Pittsburgh, 1994. A history of the Pittsburgh Section, Council of Jewish Women and Rauh's place as leader of Council.

"Under the Presidency of Mrs. Enoch Rauh, May 1903-May 1922." Historical Society of Western Pennsylvania, Library and Archives Division, Pittsburgh, PA. In 1999 Richard Enoch Rauh, grandson of Bertha Rauh, donated the Rauh family papers to The Historical Society of Western Pennsylvania (HSWP). The Historical Society's Jewish Archives has been renamed The Rauh Jewish Archives. Included in the donated archive were papers of Bertha Rauh, Enoch Rauh, Richard Rauh (son) and Richard Enoch Rauh. Bertha Rauh's papers cover the years 1904 to the 1940s.

Selavan, Ida Cohen. "Bertha Rauh, First Woman in a Mayor's Cabinet." Paper presented at Duquesne History Forum, Pittsburgh, October 12, 1981. Paper includes personal and family information. Historical Society of Western Pennsylvania.

Zugsmith, Amelia. "History of the Pittsburgh Section, Council of Jewish Women" (1919). Manuscript courtesy of University of Pittsburgh Libraries, Archive Service Center.

BOOKS

Annals of the Civic Club of Allegheny County. Vol. 2, 1914-1923. Pittsburgh: 1945.

Baum, Charlotte, Paula Hyman, and Sonya Michel. The Jewish Woman in America. New York: 1976.

Blair, Karen. Club Woman as Feminist: True Womanhood Redefined, 1868-1914. New York: 1980. Blair coined the term "domestic feminists" to describe the club women who brought home and family values to their activities outside the home.

Capone, Margaret Lynch. A History of the Allegheny County League of Women Voters: Sixty Years of Achievement. Pittsburgh: 1980.

Davis, Allen. Spearheads for Reform: The Social Settlements and the Progressive Movement, 1890-1914. New York: 1967.

Firor Scott, Anne. Natural Allies: Women's Associations in American History. Chicago: 1991.

Harper, Frank C. Pittsburgh of Today: Its Resources and People Vol. 4. New York: 1932:747.

Lord, Walter. The Good Years, 1900 To The First World War. New York: 1960. A readable account of the Progressive years in American history, particularly the optimistic conviction that any wrong in society could be righted.

Muncy, Robin. Creating a Female Dominion in American Reform, 1890-1935. Oxford: 1991.

Rogow, Faith. Gone to Another Meeting: The National Council of Jewish Women 1893-1993. Tuscaloosa, Alabama: 1993.

Sklar, Kathryn Kish. Florence Kelley and the Nation's Work: The Rise of Women's Political Culture, 1830-1900. New Haven: 1996.

ARTICLES

Esmond, Ruth. "Mrs. Enoch Rauh—Citizen," *Jewish Criterion*, November 10, 1916.

Article begins with extracts from a letter by John Brashear, "Pennsylvania's First Citizen" in which he praises the "beautiful family life" of the Rauhs.

"The Pittsburgh and Allegheny Milk and Ice Association." The Congress Outlet, Vol. 3 (October 1923).

"Who's Who in Pittsburgh Jewry." *Jewish Criterion*, March 19, 1927.

AJHS. "Rauh, Bertha (Mrs. Enoch)." AJYB, 1911-1932.

"Bertha Floersheim Rauh." Pittsburgh of Today, 1932, 747-748.

"Civic Worker 75 Years Old." *Pittsburgh Press*, 1937.

Flemington, George Thornton. "Mrs. Bertha F. Rauh." History of Pittsburgh and Environs Vol.4. New York: 1922.

"Mrs. Rauh, First Woman To Serve in a Mayor's Cabinet." *Pittsburgh Post-Gazette*, February 14, 1934.

A Review of Bertha Rauh's tenure as Director of Pittsburgh's Department of Public Welfare.

"Mrs. Enoch Rauh, Her Story." *Women's Digest,* Vol. 1, no. 2, December, 1939.

"Salute to Mrs. Enoch Rauh." *Monthly Bulletin of Pittsburgh Section, National Council of Jewish Women,* Pittsburgh, September, 1940.

Conway, Jill. "Women Reformers and American Culture, 1870-1930." *Journal of Social History* 5 (Winter 1971-72): 164-177.

Leff, Mark. "Consensus for Reform: The Mothers' Pension Movement in the Progressive Era." Social Service Review 47 (September 1973): 397–417.

Gordon, Linda. "Putting Children First: Women, Maternalism, and Welfare in the Early Twentieth Century." In U.S. History as Women's History: New Feminist Essays, edited by Linda K. Kerber, Alice Kessler-Harris and Kathryn Kish Sklar, 63–86. Chapel Hill, North Carolina: 1995.

Koven, Seth and Sonya Michel. "Womanly Duties: Maternalist Policies and the Origins of the Welfare State in France, Great Britain, and the United States, 1880–1920." American Historical Review, 95 (October 1990): 1077–1079.

Wilkinson, Patrick, "The Selfless and the Helpless: Maternalist Origins of the U.S. Welfare State." Feminist Studies (Fall 1999). Wilkinson defines "maternalism" as a "movement of middle- and upper-class women, who, between 1890 and 1930, lobbied the state to assist and protect poor mothers and working women, couching both their proposals and their own activism in an idealized rhetoric of motherhood." He discusses the paradox between activist "maternalists" who accomplished much and the feminist argument that their acts actually transferred nineteenth century gender bias to contemporary society.

Florence S. Reizenstein

(March 26, 1901–June 8, 1970)

by Lois Michaels

W ith her small but determined smile, Florence Silberstein Reizenstein fought vigorously for progressive causes. Her gentle, diminutive appearance masked one of Pittsburgh's strongest, sharpest and most widely admired advocates for legislation supporting civil rights and fair housing and labor practices, and one of the Jewish community's strongest champions for the Jewish democratic state of Israel. When she died from accidental carbon monoxide poisoning in 1970, those who mourned her death and eulogized her life came from all segments of the community—Jews and gentiles, white

(photograph courtesy of Reizenstein Family Papers, c. 1820-1990, MSS#73, Rauh Jewish Archives, Thomas and Katherine Detre Library and Archives, Senator John Heinz History Center)

people and black people, the powerful and the less powerful. During her life and after her death, this complex Jewish woman was called a "thoughtful, fiery trailblazer," a "Woman of Valor," a "jealous guardian of her privacy," a "gentle zealot" and a "champion for the black community." To one young relative, though, she was simply "fun."

Florence Winifred Silberstein was the youngest child of an upwardly mobile immigrant family. Her father, Samuel Silberstein, was the son of an Austro-Hungarian general. He ran a successful furnace and tinware business in the Homewood section of the city. He was also an inventor and gained some attention in 1897 for a compressed air motor that he believed would revolutionize streetcar travel. Her mother, Sara Tannenbaum Silberstein, managed a house in the city and a summer home on a farm near Bakerstown, Pa. and volunteered with the National Council of Jewish Women, Pittsburgh Section, during its earliest years. At a time when most Jewish families lived in posh Allegheny City or the crowded Hill District, the Silbersteins settled in Homewood, which was a relatively new and upscale suburb in the East End of the city, far from the smoky mills. They lived near the Frick family mansion and counted George Westinghouse as a friend. The parlor of their house had both an upright piano and a wind-up phonograph. Samuel and Sara Silberstein had six children—Gertrude, Sadie, Ethel, Joseph, Herschel and Florence.

A family acquaintance, Joan Brest Friedberg, said Florence came from "a generation of Americans who believed passionately that injustice could be overcome, that legislation could be enacted that would reflect the true spirit of democracy, that those who are stronger and more fortunate must work actively to open opportunities to others less favored by fate

Florence Reizenstein and her sister Sadie Alter were both active in political affairs from an early age. In the years after World War I, they jointly led the Committee on Peace and Arbitration of the National Council of Jewish Women, Pittsburgh Section. In later years, they both worked on interracial and interfaith relations. (photograph courtesy of Reizenstein Family Papers, c. 1820-1990, MSS#73, Rauh Jewish Archives, Thomas and Katherine Detre Library and Archives, Senator John Heinz History Center)

and circumstance." The Silberstein family belonged to Rodef Shalom Congregation during the tenure of Rabbi J. Leonard Levy, who was a leading voice for a socially active form of liberal Judaism. He admonished young congregants to promote the Jewish values of *tzedakah* (charity) and *gemilut chassadim* (acts of kindness). Florence took this humanitarian message to heart. When Peabody High School asked honor students to prepare talks on aspects of city government, other honorees spoke about the work of legislators and magistrates while Florence discussed "The People of Our City."

In her late teens and early twenties, Florence began her life work in community service. She volunteered for the National Council of Jewish Women, Pittsburgh Section, at a time when

Florence Reizenstein רײ

March 26, 1901–June 5, 1970

"Many daughters have done valiantly, "But thou excellest them all. . ."

Proverbs 31

Florence Reizenstein, may her memory be as a blessing.

Her tragic death leaves a wound in the Jewish community, and in the larger community, that will not soon heal. Nor, not soon will such another star rise in the social firmament which combines, in such full measure, such concern for human relations, love of Israel, and devotion to community. Mrs. Louis J. Reizenstein will ever be known as a woman who spoke her conscience, no matter the cost. She was not only the keeper of the community conscience; she was the community conscience. And, in Prophetic terms, Florence was the "still, small voice" of conscience.

In all of the storied ethic of the Jewish people, known as the "Wisdom Literature", there is drawn no more nearly perfect picture of such a one as Florence Reizenstein as has been drawn in the thirty-first chapter of Proverbs.

"A woman of valor who can find?
"Far above rubies are her worth."

A valorous woman, she, in questing every highway and by-way to plan the march toward civil rights and human rights for all, without regard for race, color, or creed.

"Her lamp goeth not out by night.
"She girds herself with strength."

Tireless she was in her efforts. She worked with vigor on behalf of the weak, the poor, the discriminated, the disadvantaged, the persecuted of her people and of her fellow peoples. She was a vigorous defender; a formidable opponent, felling an adversary with a smile and a quiet word.

"She opens her hand to the poor,
"And extends her hands to the needy."

Near and far, her gentle hand touched the fevered brow of the tempest-tossed at home, overseas, and in Israel.

"Strength and honor are her garb,
"She smiles confidently at the future."

Florence was a Lady in the purest, noblest, Jewish sense of the word. She wore dignity as though born to that robe.

And her smile, sometimes sad and gently tolerant for those who would have to learn another day, was ever-ready, humorful, and most often sunny. She knew justice must triumph. And she went about helping it, because she understood there was much work to be done against that day when the Messiah will come.

"Many daughters have done excellently,
"But thou excellest them all."

Distinguished daughter of Israel, Florence excelled in the thing we all lack most: love for the face of each human being, rather than for faceless humanity.

"Give her of the fruit of her hands,
"And let her own works praise her in the gates."

The fruit of her hands are on the branches of the Jewish tree of life.

And, her own works praise her from the gates of this city to the Gates of Eternity.

Thus, the thirty-first chapter of Proverbs pays glowing tribute to dearly beloved Florence Reizenstein — and closes the book!

When Florence Reizenstein died unexpectedly in 1970, the *Jewish Chronicle* published memorials in five successive issues, including this memoriam in the June 11, 1970 issue (documents courtesy of Pittsburgh Jewish Newspaper Project) founding members such as Bertha Rauh and Amelia Zugsmith were nearing the end of their tenures with the pioneering organization, and a new generation of leaders was emerging. She headed the National Council of Jewish Women, Pittsburgh Section's religious school, taught at the Irene Kaufmann Settlement's program for new Americans and developed an education program for organized labor. She was responsible for several innovative initiatives at the NCJW in the early 1920s. With her sister Sadie, she led the Committee on Peace and Arbitration, which was the first committee in any Jewish organization in the country devoted to the cause of world peace. As chair of the Settlement Committee, she oversaw a group of twenty volunteers who would devote an afternoon each week to "club work, teaching sewing, Sabbath school and dancing, playground leading" at the Irene Kaufmann Settlement. She also created the Clinical Committee, which trained young women to spend an afternoon each week assisting doctors at infant orthopedic clinics.

The world of Jewish philanthropy included a social element that allowed Florence to indulge her theatrical side. Younger members regularly performed plays to entertain older members at meetings and luncheons. Florence starred in one play billed as "a satire on one type of ultra-modern woman." In 1922, a reviewer in the *Jewish Criterion* specifically praised Florence's performance in another play called "The Will-O-The-Wisp," writing, "In Miss Florence Silberstein, the Waif stands out among the other characters. In fact Miss Silberstein really won the honors of the night, for her part, requiring utmost skill and dexterity, judgment and deep study, was filled with rare capability." She would later harness those same attributes in her communal work.

In 1924 Florence married Louis J. Reizenstein Jr., whose German Jewish family ran a thriving china and glassware business downtown. Instead of working in the family business, Louis took a job with a small subsidiary of the Falk family enterprises. He studied chemistry by correspondence course, invented various refining processes and started the Falk Company, which was sold to Cargill Inc. for $4 million in 1947. Florence and Louis Reizenstein had one adopted son, David, who lived in New York City for most of his adult life. The Reizensteins contributed time and money to almost every Jewish charity and also served the needs of the larger community. Their homes in Squirrel Hill and later in Shadyside became meeting places for solving problems. Sensitive to the feelings of her black guests, Florence was known to employ mostly white household help. While Florence hosted the meetings, Louis cultivated prize dahlias in his greenhouse, including one called "Red Top," after a nickname for his redheaded wife.

During the Depression years, Florence created the Pittsburgh Community Forum, where topics such as equal opportunity issues could be discussed and legislative strategies formulated. Before and during World War II she was involved in the movement for world peace and the creation of a Jewish state. She was the first president of the United Nations Association of Pittsburgh. She worked closely with David L. Lawrence while he was mayor of Pittsburgh, and this relationship became increasingly important when Lawrence was elected governor of Pennsylvania in 1959. Lawrence appointed Florence to Pittsburgh's new Human Relations Commission in 1955 and later made her the first woman to serve on the state Human Relations Commission. Their friendship was such that Lawrence accompanied Florence on a United Jewish Federation trip to Israel.

Florence used the political process to reach legislative goals. She was a master of diplomacy and persuasion and had a skill for bringing diverse groups together. She would hold closed-door meetings when necessary. Governors from both parties appointed her to state commissions, where she described her main duty to be "the administration of civil rights laws." She helped draft Fair Employment Practice Acts at the local and state level.

Among her dozens of honors, accolades and achievements, Florence is perhaps most associated with the Negro Education Emergency Drive, or NEED. Co-founded in 1963 with Marian Jordan, a black community leader, NEED was one of the first groups in Pittsburgh to provide post-high school financial aid to black students. Florence was also the first president of the Women's Division of the United Jewish Federation of Pittsburgh; an executive board member of the Pittsburgh branch of the NAACP; and a founder of Women in Urban Crisis. In 1964, she became the third person in the country to receive the Herbert Lehman Humanitarian Service Award, sponsored by Israel Bonds. That same year, Pennsylvania Governor William Scranton named Florence a Distinguished Daughter of Pennsylvania. In 1968 she received the Isabel Kennedy Award for "outstanding service in the cause of health and social welfare" from the Health and Welfare Association of the United Way of Allegheny County.

In a 1964 interview in the *Pittsburgh Press*, journalist Mary O'Hara described Florence as "a paradox... since most of her life was spent in public view, very little is known of her personally." She declined to answer questions about clothes, family and entertaining but spoke engagingly about her views on education, civil rights and Israel, a country she visited many times. She told O'Hara that she "considered the solution of racial problems to be the most challenging need of our time." That Florence also had a lighter side is apparent from a photograph of her and Louis sporting parrots on their arms.

After her death in 1970, the *Jewish Chronicle* included tributes in five consecutive issues and every major newspaper in the city published a remembrance. That year, the Pittsburgh Human Rights Commission established an award in her memory. In 1975, the Pittsburgh Board of Education named its newest school after her. (Reizenstein Middle School was demolished in 2012.) Almost a decade after her death, NEED Executive Director Dr. Herbert Reid Jr. told the *Chronicle*, "It is too bad for us all that Florence Reizenstein is not still alive. Florence is the one person in this town who knew how to get inter-community communication going, and to keep it going to achieve results."

SOURCES:

Reizenstein, Louis, oral history interview, 1974, *Pittsburgh and Beyond: the Experience of the Jewish Community,* National Council of Jewish Women, Pittsburgh Section, Oral History Collection at the University of Pittsburgh (http://images.library.pitt.edu/cgi-bin/i/image/image-idx?view=entry;cc=ncjw;entryid=x-ais196440.363)

Reizenstein Family Papers, c. 1820-1990, MSS#73, Rauh Jewish Archives, Thomas and Katherine Detre Library and Archives, Senator John Heinz History Center

Reizenstein Family Photographic Collection, c. 1860-1970, MSP#73, Rauh Jewish Archives, Thomas and Katherine Detre Library and Archives, Senator John Heinz History Center

"Temple Players," *Jewish Criterion,* January 20, 1922, p. 18

Miriam Schonfield

(November 2, 1888–January 25, 1934)

by Ruth C. Reidbord

E ducation has always been of utmost importance throughout Jewish history. That usually meant men studying
sacred texts. Occasionally women, particularly the daughters
of rabbis, were given limited opportunities to study with
their fathers, but this was not the norm. Jewish women
found some opportunities for learning; in fact we know of
Hebrew and Yiddish poetry written by women, dating back
several hundred years. But a Jewish woman educator? Rather
unusual. Even more astounding is that the first principal of
the Columbian Council School in Pittsburgh was a woman,
aged 20: Miriam Schonfield.

(photograph courtesy of Miriam Schonfield Photographs, Thomas and
Katherine Detre Library and Archives, Senator John Heinz History Center)

Miriam Schonfield was born in Zanesville, Ohio on November 2, 1888, to Louis and Hannah Nathan Schonfield. Her father was born in Germany and became a wholesale clothing merchant. Her mother was born in England but moved with her family to Philadelphia, where she taught in the Jewish Temple Religious School until she married. The family moved to Pittsburgh when Miriam was eight years old. She resided in Pittsburgh the rest of her life. The family lived first on Darlington Road in the 6200 block and then some members, including Miriam, moved to 5222 Forbes Avenue, near Margaret Morrison Street. Miriam graduated from Allegheny High School and attended both the Margaret Morrison Carnegie School for Women at the Carnegie Institute of Technology (now Carnegie Mellon University) and the Pennsylvania College for Women (now Chatham University). There is no evidence she graduated from either college. She had two sisters, Carrie Schonfield Loeb and Olivia Schonfield, and two brothers, J. L. Schonfield, who moved to Buffalo, New York, and Dr. Moses Schonfield.

Miriam Schonfield started her career as a Jewish educator at the Center Avenue Religious School in 1899, when she was eleven. With the help of the Columbian Council of Jewish Women (later called the National Council of Jewish Women, Pittsburgh Section, or NCJW) and Rodef Shalom Congregation, particularly its Sisterhood, she developed the Southwestern District of Pennsylvania Jewish Religious Schools, a regional system of religious schools that lasted for 30 years after her death. It began in the Hill District, where most Jews in Pittsburgh lived at the time. In 1908 it expanded into other parts of the city and into neighboring communities. At its height in the 1920's, the system had 60 schools, 325 teachers and 3,000 students. The office of the Field Supervisor, the top administrative post, was in Miss Schonfield's home. Under her direction, the program expanded into some unexpected places, including the Morganza and Thornhill "correctional institutions" and the Western Pennsylvania School for the Deaf. She hosted Teachers Institutes every month at Rodef Shalom. These became a venue for young Jewish men and women to socialize, something she thought very important. Some of her schools became the nuclei of new congregations.

One of her many innovations was the Mothers Clubs she would form before starting a new school. These provided a support network for the school and also educated the largely immigrant mothers about the need for Jewish educa-tion—not just *cheder* for their sons. Miss Schonfield recog-nized that mothers were the backbone of the family and the force needed to gain support for the schools. For example, the school in Braddock had 175 students enrolled in 1921, with a Mother's Club of 175. The school put on several plays throughout the year, and the talent evinced by the students was a "revelation to the people of Braddock. The attendance at one of these plays at the Carnegie Music Hall of Braddock was approximately 1,500."

Miss Schonfield was not content to sit in her home office on Darlington Road to administer the program. Each week, and sometimes three times on Sunday, she would travel to the schools by public transportation to give instructions in how to study and what to study, since curriculum devel-opment was in its infancy at the time. In 1923 she visited 20 schools to instruct individually and through monthly Teachers Institutes.

Another of Miss Schonfield's innovations was to provide a Jewish religious school experience for children of all denominations and backgrounds. To quote the 1925 NCJW annual report, "This District (of NCJW) is best known for its... religious schools. Some have asserted that this is the function of the synagogue, not the Council. But it must be borne in mind that this program reaches all phases of Judaism. It does not advocate Reform, Conservative or Orthodox. It offers Judaism in whatever form the community desires, our only stipulation is that the teaching be in English. Hebrew instruction can be and often is supplementary... Most of our teachers are drawn from the ranks of students in local colleges and receive personal instruction from Miss Schonfield. There is stimulation towards things essentially Jewish and spiritual."

Many teachers in the program later said that Miss Schonfield had a way of drawing people to her that subsequent administrators lacked. "Those who knew Miss Schonfield never forgot her. To be in her presence was a rare privilege. She cared about everyone and remembered everyone's names. The Teachers Institute she organized was virtually the only opportunity for young people in outlying areas to meet other young Jewish people... She was so inspiring that these young teachers worked for no pay, receiving only money for 'carfare,'" one of the teachers, Grace Fivars, later recalled.

The only report written by Miss Schonfield extant is her annual report for 1927/1928. In it, she wrote, "In our schools this year, we have tried not only to impart knowledge, but to deepen faith. We have taught the children history and the ideals and principles and ethics of our religion, so that they could translate it into life... We have asked our mothers in our districts to teach the children to pray and to recall the

In 1916, as the Southwestern District of Pennsylvania Jewish Religious Schools program was nearing its height, Miriam Schonfield wrote a brief reminiscences of the early days of the program for the *Jewish Criterion*. (documents courtesy of Pittsburgh Jewish Newspaper Project)

RELIGIOUS SCHOOLS COMMITTEE OF C. J. U.

REMINISCENCES.

By Miss Miriam Schonfield, Chairman of Printing, Chairman of Industrial Display, Secretary of Religious Schools Committee.

To one who has had the opportunity to observe from the inside over a number of years, the achievements of our Section of the Council of Jewish Women, a wonderful inspiration comes from the work of those who have gone before as well as from that of those who are to-day giving so much of themselves to carry on the tasks that have been so well inaugurated.

The Council enters into and touches every human activity that is of vital importance to the welfare and aggrandizement of the Jewish people. Throughout the years of its existence the catholicity of its principals, the high altruism of its ideals, and the broad basis of its humanity have preserved it inviolate against the attacks of those who, actuated by various selfish motives, have attempted to deprecate its actual accom-out of chaos have come order and harmony, enthusiasm and true Council the spirit which strives:

plishments. The limitation of time does not permit the recitation of all its good work, neither does my ability suffice to enumerate and explain all of the fields of activity which have been so fertile in results. I shall, therefore, content myself at this time with merely touching upon the more definite impressions that I have received from that part of the work with which I have been most closely allied.

I would like to take you back with me to the first religious school started by the Council, and then show you how in the space of a few years this school has been the incentive for the establishment by the Council of more schools year by year, until now there are enrolled under our banner nineteen well established and progressive schools for the teaching of the Jewish religion to children who otherwise would have no opportunity of understanding to the best advantage the tenets of our faith. This first school in itself was the nucleus of what is now the Settlement School, and although it is not now under the direction of the Council, the influence of the

early Council members who worked in and for the school is still felt through all the years of its growth.

In considering what is best for its people, the Council has never lost sight of the fact that one of its most obvious duties is to help dispel that ever-present prejudice that is held by the unknowing toward the Jew. Many have been its methods of Education of these prejudiced minds but one activity has helped so much along this line that it deserves special mention. I refer to the Industrial Display, which has always been non-sectarian in character. All of the philanthropic and charitable institutions as well as individuals whose handiwork is a means of their support, are invited to display their work under our guidance. The various articles are then not only displayed but also sold by the Council at its Display, and all the proceeds are turned over to the makers of the articles. So much favorable comment has been elicited through this because of the altruistic spirit displayed, that this work must be considered as one of the Council's notable achievements.

One of the most interesting lines of work that it has been my privilege to enjoy was that connected with the Playground Association. As a representative of the Council, I was affiliated with this association. Much, indeed, do playgrounds mean to these children of the streets, our future citizens; and truly it can be said that one of the pioneers in this so important movement in our community was the Pittsburgh Section of the Council of Jewish Women.

And then the Summer Camp for Working Girls. I cannot possibly close without mentioning this recently inaugurated method of providing recreation and pleasure for those Jewish girls who all the year round must work so hard in our stores and factories. True it is that the posibilities of this work have not been developed with the broadness and scope which it really deserves, but it is one of the newer phases of Council activity and without a doubt will some day develop into a wonderful institution. Even as it was last year, and I speak advisedly, as I was in direct charge of the Camp, the amount of good in pleas-

ure, health and recreation for the small number of girls for which we were able to provide can only be estmiated by those who personally came in contact with the Camp during its progress.

To most of my readers, the remarkably valuable work of the Council is well known. As a result of its untiring efforts, individually and collectively, its members have been made more useful to society. Too much credit cannot be given to its officers and active members in having accomplished so much in the comparatively short time which it has been in existence. Much, however, remains to be done. It is within the province of the Council to promulgate the standards of its activities; but after all it is in the appreciation of its efforts by the public that the amount of its success is measured.

It is to be hoped then that the future will rob all uncalled for antagonism of its sting and that all unjust opposition removed, the Pittsburgh Section, Council of Jewish Women, will hold its rightful place as the leading Jewish organization in the city.

lesson to the children during the week, thus helping the children to remember what they have learned." Note that Miss Schonfield placed her entire emphasis on the mother's role in the child's Jewish education. This is a notable departure from the traditional model and could be seen as an inspiration for Jewish feminists. Miss Schonfield, who never married, understood the central role that women play in the life of young children.

The program changed after Miss Schonfield died in 1934. In professionalizing the program, later administrators lost the warmth and intimacy that Miss Schonfield had brought to the endeavor. She understood the needs of underserved children and communities and, as a long-time Pittsburgher, the dynamics of small town communities.

Although Miriam Schonfield devoted the greatest portion of her adult life to the Southwestern District school system, she also led a relatively well-rounded life as a patron of the arts, a civic leader and a club woman. We find many examples of her interest in theater in her scrapbook. We also learn that she was active in efforts to prepare for America's entrance into the First World War, always working within the framework of established women's organizations, both Jewish and secular. She also founded a summer camp for working girls near Wexford that was sponsored by NCJW.

But her desire to help young people was poignantly illustrated by an article in the *Pittsburgh Post-Gazette* in 1931. "A tall bewildered boy sat in the best arm chair in the living room of Miss Miriam Schonfield's home on Forbes Street... He was a freshman at the University," the reporter wrote. "Before him he could see only dismal failure so he had come to talk over his problems with Miss Schonfield whom he knew had helped others. He said, in a letter he wrote to her a few months later, 'I left that evening with a new view towards life and my fellowmen. You took my worries and my distorted attitude towards the world and returned soothing advice and wise council.'

"He was only one of the hundreds of young people whom Miss Schonfield has inspired with her optimism and courage. Boys and girls all over the city, especially the members of the nine Jewish fraternities at the University of Pittsburgh and Carnegie Tech know that as long as they see the light burning on the porch of her home she will be glad to talk with them."

In ancient times there were Jewish women who led their communities. But as religion was formalized, men took over and silenced women's voices. Miriam Schonfield reclaimed an important role for women, even though she was unaware that was what she was doing. A very traditional woman, she lived a non-traditional life that inspired Jewish men and women for decades after she passed from the scene. She would have been happy to know this. In 1915 she wrote that the justification for starting a movement and allowing someone else to carry it on had a precedent in the uncompleted work of Moses. This from a woman named Miriam. How appropriate: Moses' sister!

[Author's note: This paper is dedicated to my mother, Anne Schiff Cooper, z'l who was instrumental in founding the Kiski Valley Religious School, affiliated with the Southwestern District of Pennsylvania Jewish Religious Schools and who inspired me to study and love all things Jewish. Thanks to Susan M. Melnick, archivist at the Rauh Jewish Archives of the Heinz History Center and Martha Berg, archivist of Rodef Shalom Congregation.]

SOURCES:

"Personals: Irene Kaufmann Settlement," *Jewish Criterion*, December 20, 1912, p. 15

National Council of Jewish Women, Pittsburgh Section Papers, 1894-2011, AIS.1964.40, Archives Service Center, University of Pittsburgh

"Miss Schonfield Enjoys Social Service Work," by Anna Jane Phillips, *Pittsburgh Post-Gazette*, April 9, 1931, p. 11

"Southwestern District of Pennsylvania Jewish Religious Schools," Ruth Cooper Reidbord in *Pursuing Peace Across the Alleghenies: The Rodef Shalom Congregation, 1856-2005,* Walter Jacob, Editor, Rodef Shalom Press, Pittsburgh, Pennsylvania, 2005.

Corinne Azen Krause Papers, 1845- 2002, MSS#113, Rauh Jewish Archives, Thomas and Katherine Detre Library and Archives, Senator John Heinz History Center

Frieda Goldstein Shapira

(March 7, 1914–July 7, 2003)

by Edie Shapira

F rieda Goldstein Shapira brought the spirit of a social worker to the non-profit community and beyond. She was known for being a highly engaged board member who attended meetings, studied issues and asked insightful questions. She was particularly admired for being able to build bridges. Her friends reflected a rich tapestry of diversity.

Her father, Joseph Goldstein, grew up in downtown Pittsburgh. His mother had died during childbirth when he was three, and his grandmother raised him. After graduating from Fifth Avenue High School, he got a job as a billing clerk for a Penn Avenue grocery wholesaler. He soon became

(photograph courtesy of *Jewish Chronicle* Photographs, Thomas and Katherine Detre Library and Archives, Senator John Heinz History Center)

a successful traveling salesman for the company. Following World War I, he joined two of his customers and became a partner in the Eagle Grocery Company, which grew to 125 stores and sold out to Kroger in 1928. Three years later, Goldstein joined the OK Grocery Company, owned by two other immigrant Jewish men. His former partners also joined, and OK Grocery grew to become the Giant Eagle Inc. supermarket chain, one of the largest privately held companies in America. Joseph Goldstein was interested in politics from an early age and often attended meetings of Jewish Socialist groups in the Hill District. While sympathetic to their causes, he believed change would only occur through the existing political structure, Frieda Shapira recalled in an oral history with the National Council of Jewish Women, Pittsburgh Section. Every Friday night, after asking his children about their schoolwork, he engaged them in vigorous political conversations and encouraged them to try to change his views.

Frieda's mother, Dora Bornstein Goldstein, immigrated to Pittsburgh from Ukraine in 1903, after her father had abandoned the family. She attended night classes at the Council House and earned $3 a week as a bookkeeper for Singer Sewing Machines on Penn Avenue in downtown. She was exceptionally cultured, filling her home with books and music and taking every opportunity to attend the theatre and opera. Although English was her second language, she spoke more properly than her native husband, who learned how to speak on the streets of the city.

In contrast to her parents, Frieda was born into a stable and loving family. She was the oldest of three children. The family lived for a short time on Cliff Street, in the Hill District, before moving to a rented house in Point Breeze and eventually buying a house on Hobart Street in Squirrel Hill. They were one of the first families on their block to buy a car and take vacations. Joe was full of warmth, wit and humor. Dora was a devoted mother and homemaker. One of her treats was cookie dough topped with butter, sugar, nuts and cinnamon. She called these FML cakes, after her children: Frieda, Morris and Leah. The family was active at Congregation B'nai Israel and observed the Sabbath and major Jewish holidays. They were also proud Americans. They traveled, attended cultural events, and encouraged all three of their children to pursue higher education.

Frieda's senior class was among the first to graduate from Allderdice High School in Squirrel Hill. She earned a bachelor's degree from the University of Pittsburgh. In 1934, she married a classmate, Saul Shapira, whom she had come to know well through the undergraduate debate team. The two were full intellectual partners and perfectly aligned in their values, interests and deep commitment to improving the community. They both understood discrimination first hand. Saul had wanted to become a political science professor but decided to study law after a guidance counselor told him that universities rarely hired Jews. Once, they were turned away from a resort because of their ethnicity. Together, they attended Columbia University, in New York. Frieda earned a degree in social work, and when they returned to Pittsburgh she supervised children in foster homes and worked with neglected children through the Children's Service Bureau, a forerunner of the Allegheny County Office of Children, Youth, and Families. Saul briefly practiced law before joining the newly created Pittsburgh Housing Authority, one of the first public housing agencies in the country. It was

Frieda Shapira was skilled at using boards and committees to establish relationships and create change. Her volunteer work began during the rapid social changes of the 1960s. She is seen here with Mayor Joseph Barr. (photograph courtesy of The Frieda and Saul Shapira Papers, 1935-2003, MSS#508, Rauh Jewish Archives, Thomas and Katherine Detre Library and Archives, Senator John Heinz History Center)

idealistic and exciting work, which is why the couple felt "great trepidation" when Goldstein asked Saul to join Giant Eagle. Ultimately, though, Saul left the housing agency in 1945 to work for his father-in-law. Saul, with his law degree, was the first person in the company to have graduated from college. In 1968, he succeeded Goldstein to become the second president of the company.

Frieda initially stayed home to raise her four children. She loved motherhood and found it deeply satisfying. Yet she remained engaged in the issues of the day. Her early community work took place within the Jewish community.

In June 2000, Winchester Thurston School asked Frieda Shapira to deliver a charge for its graduating class, which included her granddaughter. In her speech (seen here in manuscript form), she advised the students to pursue their passions and to seek out people from different backgrounds. (documents courtesy of the Shapira family)

Graduation — Commencement

2 words meaning different things
and yet they name the same event.

You have just graduated from high
school and you are commencing a new life
Is it a relief to be finished here? Yes
Is it scary to start something new? Yes
It's scary and oh so exciting.

Some of you are going to schools far
away. Some are going to school in Pgh.
(but not to live at home, Heaven forbid)
and some are going to take time off from
school for a while and test themselves in
the real world of work.

Each one of these choices will
shape you in becoming adults and
living your lives to the fullest.

And that was going to be the gist of
my message. Living life to the full,
fullest which to me means participation
in the world beyond yourselves.

Family, friends and career are the
most important elements of ones life
Sometimes anyone of these can be consuming, shutting out other interests.
Careers especially can be consuming. There
is a lot of talent in this room. I was particularly interested in seeing the newest
edition of your literary magazine, "Plaid",
full of originality, creativity and beauty
A few of you will make it to the
top in your chosen careers. Most of us

2

will live our lives unnoticed by the media.

But living life to the fullest, participating in the world beyond us doesn't depend on the media, or fame, or money.

It means getting to know people different from ourselves, it means embracing causes that might make the world a better place, it means learning where people hurt and trying to find ways to relieve that hurt, It means learning what is great about our community, and supporting that greatness, it means learning what is wrong with our community and trying to find answers.

Most of you have already tasted a little of this. Winchester Thurston has created opportunities for you to achieve beyond yourselves. You know that there are hungry people and you have collected food for them. You have tutored students who are having trouble with school work, and you have volunteered in hospitals. All these are a beginning.

One day you will become aware of a social need or injustice that catches your attention in a way that makes you want to help. You will want to find out more about it. You will start talking with others who have the same interest. You will start being a player. You will be on a team of people who share your ideals and dreams about the world. They will be people whom you would never

3

meet in your daily schedule.

They will be richer than you and poorer than you, they will be of different religions and nationality backgrounds But they will be interested in the same problems you are interested in and it is so much fun to get to know them and call them friends.

And as I said before, you will have become a player, not a bystander You will make difference in your world, change it (hopefully for the better although we can't always be sure it will be better)

But you will have lived it, participated in it, learned from it and be changed by it

For me this is living life to the fullest. We talk about doing good for others, by giving back to the community if we have been blessed with many of the good things of life. All that is noble and compassionate But it will also enrich you in more ways than I can count It will bring you satisfaction & friendship and happiness

I said I wouldn't preach but I can't resist from saying that you have options and if you can find a way to use your unique personality & ability in some activity or cause that you think is important then go for it. It won't be enough to sit in the grandstand or watch on TV or be unaware there

4

es. even a game. You will be in the
field, living life to the fullest.
I got into this without pre planning.
When I started having children I
left work to stay home & raise them.
~~Everyone~~ Many women did that then.
Few women do that today. When you
are ready to have children who knows?

When my youngest child was 11.
I became very active in an organization that had a community service
program and an advocacy program
on social issues. We wanted to do
something in the field of education
and were advised by the ~~Pgh~~ Public
Schools psychologist that ~~the~~
professional educators were looking to
pre-school education. This was around
[early 1960's]
1960 & no one ever heard of Headstart.
Several of us went to the Bd of Ed and
discussed with them the possibility of
getting 3 & 4 yr olds into the public
schools. They had never done this before
but they were interested. They had
kindergartens but recognized that
many children came to school unpre-
pared for kinderten. So they gave us
rooms in 9 schools in the poorest
neighborhoods of the city. We got 100
volunteers practically overnight, a
number of them former school teachers. We
arranged a 6 lecture course on the
culture & attitudes of the Afro American
community, by an Afro American

5

social worker. One of the former school teachers cried because she learned how little she understood her former African American pupils and how little she had expected of them. The former Ford Foundation was interested and gave the funds to pay regular teachers in each classroom & our volunteers became assistants, each working one or two sessions a week.

most chn at risk are white our group was confined realize later

The program was called the Cultural Enrichment Program and lasted several years. Other cities across the country were trying similar demonstrations and it was soon apparent that 3 & 4 yr olds were more ready to learn in kindergarten & first grade than children not given this opportunity.

Testimony was presented to Congress and the Head Start program was created. *what preceded Head Start the origins* Few people still remember the origins, but the volunteers who participated have the tremendous satisfaction of knowing they were there players.

School failure is a national crisis. The percentage of our population that can't read well or do math well never make in the new world of computers & websites. *the largest number of these is white the* A lot of research has been done on the brain development of babies. It is now known that from the moment of birth, loving attention, verbal stimulation, music are essential to the formation of brain connectors activities and

6

that waiting till a child is 3 is too late.

So how to address this to parents who are themselves too uneducated, too young, too poor in money & spirit to understand this?

One principle we have learned is you can't go into a community with a different culture than your own and say "Here is how you need to live." They won't listen to you.

Change has to come from within the community, the parent or the child. And here is the great challenge. How to convey what we know to be essential for intellectual & social development to others who maybe hostile, suspicious, or disinterested.

To lessen the gap between the poor & the rich, the educated and the unskilled is where the action is. Whoever can address this in any way, successfully or unsuccessfully will be living life to the fullest.

I hope that at some stage in your lives, not when you are studying for exams or are engaged in your establishing yourselves in your careers, or are giving all your energy to family responsibilities, but at some time you will find that you can be a player in addressing the key challenges of our country.

7

I am honored to have been chosen to give
this address. I am now 86 yrs old &
still going strong. When I reflect upon
my life I have discovered a ~~reason~~ ✗
that I am sharing with you.
That I and ~~the people I have~~
~~known~~ people I know, including me,
~~The ones who have achieved happiness~~
~~That to achieve happiness~~
~~including me are the people who~~
~~have fulfilled all their potential~~
~~and your life goal~~

In order for you to achieve
happiness in your life you have
to able to look at yourself and say
that you fulfilled all of your
potential

✗   that I and the people I have
               who are
known ~~are~~ are the happiest are those
who have fulfilled their potential
by ~~putting~~ engaging their abilities in ~~a world~~ causes
~~larger~~ bigger than themselves.

She polled political candidates on behalf of the National Council of Jewish Women, Pittsburgh Section, and she was public policy chair for the Temple Sinai Sisterhood. With NCJW, she helped launch what later became the early childhood education program Head Start, initiated a free lunch program in city schools and, as a board member of Women in Community Service, she helped establish one of the first nonresidential Job Corps centers for women in the country—Congress had initially approved the training program only for men. She was president of the local NCJW chapter from 1966 to 1968, during which time she helped launch a pioneering oral history project of the Jewish community. She came to believe that social equality for African Americans was the most important issue facing the country. Among her papers is a letter, on NCJW stationery, addressed to President John F. Kennedy, encouraging him to pass the strongest possible version of civil rights legislation.

Over time, Frieda's involvement and influence extended far beyond the Jewish community. She sat on the boards of dozens of non-profits and agencies, including the United Way of Allegheny County, the YWCA of Greater Pittsburgh, the United Jewish Federation, the University of Pittsburgh and WQED. Among her favorites were the Forbes Fund and Pittsburgh Foundation, where she served for 18 years and became vice-chair. "Being in that position, in those two organizations, I sort of feel that I'm at the pulse of everything going on in town. And I just enjoy it. I'm not doing this to be good or to get anything. I enjoy it more than playing bridge or playing golf. I just love this kind of activity. It has just become my life," she said in a 1992 oral history interview with the NCJW.

In 2000, at 86 years old, Frieda explained her philosophy for living and working in a graduation address at Winchester Thurston School, where one of her granddaughters was a graduate. She told the students, "One day you will become aware of a social need or injustice that catches your attention in a way that makes you want to help. You will want to find out more about it. You will start being a team player. You will start talking with others who have the same interest. You will be on a team of people who share your ideals and dreams about the world. They will be people whom you would never meet in your daily schedule. They will be richer than you and poorer than you. They will be of different religions and nationality backgrounds. But they will be interested in the same problems you are interested in and it is so much fun to get to know them and call them friends. You will have become a player, not a bystander. You will make a difference in your world."

[Editors' note: Edie Shapira is a daughter of Frieda Shapira]

SOURCES:

Shapira, Frieda, oral history interview, 1979, *Pittsburgh and Beyond: the Experience of the Jewish Community,* National Council of Jewish Women, Pittsburgh Section, Oral History Collection at the University of Pittsburgh (http://images.library.pitt.edu/cgi-bin/i/image/image-idx?view=entry;cc=ncjw;entryid=x-ais196440.416)

Shapira, Frieda, oral history interview, 1992, *Pittsburgh and Beyond: the Experience of the Jewish Community,* National Council of Jewish Women, Pittsburgh Section, Oral History Collection at the University of Pittsburgh (http://images.library.pitt.edu/cgi-bin/i/image/image-idx?view=entry;cc=ncjw;entryid=x-ais196440.415)

"A Pittsburgh Century: The Shapira Family," by Sally Kalson, *Pittsburgh Post-Gazette,* March 30, 1999, p. H-8

The Frieda and Shapira Papers, 1935-2003, MSS#508, Rauh Jewish Archives, Thomas and Katherine Detre Library and Archives, Senator John Heinz History Center

National Council of Jewish Women, Pittsburgh Section Papers, 1894-2011, AIS.1964.40, Archives Service Center, University of Pittsburgh

Taking flight: the story of Giant Eagle, by Mary Brignano, Giant Eagle, 2008

Barbara Kramer Shore

(November 26, 1920–October 23, 2013)

by Joan Shames

By combining scholarship with a charitable spirit, Dr. Barbara K. Shore greatly expanded the influence of social work in Western Pennsylvania. She was known as a consensus builder for her ability to unite diverse groups of people in common cause and also for her commitment to connecting the academic and practical sides of her profession.

Barbara Kramer was born in Squirrel Hill in 1920. Her grandparents had immigrated to Western Pennsylvania in the 1880s from Eastern Europe and settled in the Hill District. One grandfather worked for Frank & Seder Department Store and another ran a shop on Vickroy Street. Her parents, Cecelia

(photograph courtesy of Joan Shames)

and Benjamin Kramer, met through social activities in the Hill District and moved to Squirrel Hill after their wedding.

Growing up in Squirrel Hill, Shore was part of a tight-knit Jewish community that was exposed to the wider gentile world on a daily basis. Her parents spoke Yiddish to each other but English to their children. The family attended Rodef Shalom Congregation, which was decidedly Americanized in the Reform tradition. A gifted musician from an early age, Shore took piano lessons from a nun at Saint Philomena Church on Forward Avenue, which she said became "a real scandal" among her Jewish friends in Squirrel Hill. Her father ran B.M. Kramer & Company, a mill and mine supply business on the South Side. He was one of the few Jews in the field. He was also a "baseball fiend" who not only took his children to see the Pittsburgh Pirates at Forbes Field but also to Negro League games when the region hosted two beloved franchises.

Shore said she first heard the word "Jew" at the age of five, when Catholic neighbors informed her that Jews were "Christ-killers," and she later recalled being chased through the streets of Squirrel Hill by a young girl who called her a "dirty Jew." (The neighbor later apologized when the women met again in college.) On Shore's first day of college, an administrator pulled all the Jewish students aside to warn them against being "clannish." With many fraternities, sororities and other student groups being closed to Jews during her early years of college, Shore and many other Jews flocked to the *Carnegie Tartan*, a student newspaper. She started as a copy editor and eventually became news editor. At the paper, she also met her future husband, Jack Shore.

Shore attended Colfax elementary school and Allderdice High School. She had decided she wanted to be a social worker at an early age. She was drawn to the profession by the example of two women. Her paternal grandmother was active in the Lechem Aniyum (Bread for the Poor) Society and the Hebrew Burial Society in the Hill District. Her mother had worked as a visiting nurse under Anna B. Heldman at the Irene Kaufmann Settlement House from her high school days until she started a family. Shore graduated from the social work program at Margaret Morrison Carnegie College for Women at the Carnegie Institute of Technology, which is now Carnegie Mellon University. She earned a master's degree in social work at the University of Pittsburgh.

Barbara Shore was raised in Pittsburgh and joined the University of Pittsburgh in the 1960s, first as a student and later as a professor in its School of Social Work. She became one of the most distinguished members of the faculty, in any department, and is seen here in her role as the grand marshal of the University of Pittsburgh commencement activities in 1987. (photograph courtesy of Joan Shames)

Soon thereafter, the Shores moved to Chicago, where Jack Shore was attending graduate school. To complete her certification in the field, Shore spent a little more than a year working at the Chicago State Hospital, which required a three-hour daily commute. She later took a position at the Jewish Children's Bureau, specifically its Marks Nathan Jewish Orphan Home. This was a time when traditional orphanages across the country were being closed in favor of foster care or small group homes. Shore was responsible for finding temporary homes for children whose parents were unable to provide care. As that project neared completion, Shore became responsible for approximately 150 young Jewish men who had been freed from Nazi concentration camps at the end of World War II.

After leaving Chicago in 1947, Shore put her career on hold for 13 years to raise her four children—Erica, Deborah, David and Benita. The Shores lived in upstate New York, where Jack Shore continued his education and career, before returning to Pittsburgh in 1950. They were among the first Jewish families to live in the newly developed Stanton Heights neighborhood of the city. During those years, she did "huge amounts" of volunteering with Hadassah, the Irene Kaufmann Center (where she played violin), the Stanton Heights Recreation Program and particularly the Sunnyside Elementary School Parent-Teacher Association. As PTA president, she pushed the school to serve lunch, which freed mothers to work during the day. In 1961, after her youngest child started school, she took a part-time job as a caseworker with Travelers Aid.

Eager to teach, Shore returned to the University of Pittsburgh. In the mid-1960s, she simultaneously enrolled in a doctoral program in social work and in a master's program in the Graduate School of Public Health. She finished both degrees in the early 1970s. When an interviewer expressed admiration for the energy it must have taken to pursue two degrees while raising four children, Shore said, "Well, that's what it took."

After completing her doctorate, Shore joined the faculty at the University of Pittsburgh School of Social Work, where she remained until she retired. During her tenure, she led the Doctoral Program at the School of Social Work for almost 20 years, wrote more than 50 papers and book chapters, co-authored two books and consulted across the country and around the world. She was president of the University Senate three times and served on numerous University committees and task forces. Upon her retirement, in 1992, the University of Pittsburgh named her a Distinguished Service Professor. The university created two anti-discrimination related awards in her honor.

Her professional interests focused on women, children, aging and the disabled but seemed to include all marginalized groups in society in one way or another. In the late 1980s and early 1990s, she headed an Allegheny County task force to study Children and Youth Services and later oversaw implementation of her recommendations. She helped launch the Single Women in Midlife Crisis project of the NCJW Pittsburgh Section, the Allegheny County Rape Crisis Center, the Persad Center for Services to Gay and Lesbian Persons and the Children's Lobby of Western Pennsylvania. Shore served on more than thirty boards and task forces during her long career. "I've really always tried to build a linkage between professional social work and academia, and what goes on in the field out there," Shore said in a National Council of Jewish Women, Pittsburgh Section, oral history in 1993.

What makes

Barbara Shore run?

To an outsider,
it's a lifelong commitment to service.
To her, it's simply...

"The most exciting thing in the world"

Barbara Shore juggles an armload of papers and books and struggles to unlock her office door. It's perhaps the longest she will stand in one place all day.

Door mastered, she swoops in and turns on lights all around the room. Feeds her fish. Gives her secretary a chapter of her latest book — on aging and mental health — for typing. Sips Roy Rogers coffee and applies jelly to a bagel while skimming through the papers stacked on every flat or semi-flat surface (bookshelf, desk, file cabinet, typewriter, underneath framed photos of her children and grandchildren).

The stacks have stabilized a little since July 1, when Shore wrapped up a two-year term as president of the University Senate, the body of faculty, key administrators, and student leaders that shares in the governance of the University. But she moved right on to co-chairing the senate's committee on tenure and academic freedom. And then there's her work as director of the doctoral program for the School of Social Work. Of course she teaches, too — including an enormously popular course on death and dying that attracts future doctors, nurses, and psychologists as well as social-work students.

A new book tops the stacks: 489 *Hardworking Women, A Directory for Pennsylvania.* Yes, Barbara Shore is in it. The only wonder is that she didn't write it, too.

"I do have a high energy level," she allows between bites of bagel. "I don't need sleep a lot, never have. That helps considerably."

In fact, Shore's campus activities are only the tip of the fireball. She recently chaired a task force to recommend improvements in Allegheny County's Office of Children and Youth Services; the *Pittsburgh Post-Gazette* cited the results as proof that change for the better in government is possible. Shore works as a consultant on death and dying for the Contact Crisis Line. She helps employees prepare for retirement at such corporations as PPG, Mellon Bank, and Koppers. She recently completed a two-year term as chair of the Pennsylvania Medical Education Licensing Board — the first consumer representative to chair a Pennsylvania regulatory board and only the second non-

medical member in the nation to head a medical licensing board.

Shore charted this busy path for herself long ago. "I've wanted to be a social worker since as far back as I can remember," she says. While other kids dreamed of becoming fire fighters or cowpokes, Shore heard stories from her mother of her work in a settlement house in Pittsburgh's Hill District — and decided helping others is "the most exciting thing in the world to do."

She earned both her masters and doctorate from Pitt's School of Social Work — plus a masters from the Graduate School of Public Health. A faculty member since 1965, Shore has made her mark particularly in research relating to women and the elderly.

In 1978, she became the chief researcher for a major federally funded study of the long-term consequences of rape. More recently, Shore and colleague Martha Baum received a research grant to look at the impact of unemployment on women of the Mon Valley. Shore says, "I'm interested in how people deal with women and their development and needs, in supporting women to help them achieve the most that they can achieve."

Of her work with issues of aging, Shore says, "It's the growth industry of them all. What's exciting about it is that our time is a first in human history — there are no precedents to guide us. We have never had as many older people. We have never had as many older people living as long as they do.

"Historically, it's been a field of no interest. We don't really like aging; we've had a youth culture. Funding for research until recently has been minimal. So it's a wide-open field."

Shore leans forward in her chair as if the future is giving her a push. "All it takes is brains and money to begin to get approaches to these problems," she goes on. "With good brains put to a task and money for support, we can solve problems we've never paid any attention to before."

She has been doing a lot of thinking about both money and the future lately: As senate president, she has also chaired Pitt's Internal Campaign — the Annual Giving Fund (AGF) effort that seeks support from the University community. Shore notes the rapid progress the campaign has made in raising funds from faculty, staff, retirees, and volunteers: Last year Pitt's Internal Campaign topped its $240,000 goal.

"I don't take personal credit," she quickly adds. "We've had a great committee and staff."

Shore sees the impact of donations right in the School of Social Work, where AGF monies help pay for scholarships. But continued growth in the Internal Campaign is also crucial for its symbolic effect: "It's a very strong argument for *external* support, to be able to demonstrate *internal* support."

Ultimately, it's a matter of investing in the future. Shore believes the return — both for Pitt and its wider constituencies — can be substantial.

"I'm very committed to the notion that people in the academic arena have a great deal to offer in community service," she says. "We say very glibly that service is the third leg of the stool — teaching, research, and service — but we need to increase the impact of the University on the community.

"It's clear that the University is responding to this need — helping Western Pennsylvania make the transition from a basic steel area to whatever we might become. That should not be in *contradiction* to our basic research and teaching mission, but rather *in concert with* it. It's all of a piece."

Doubt it? Barbara Shore is living — and very busy — proof.
— DAVID A. FRYXELL

"I'm very committed to the notion that people in the academic arena have a great deal to offer in community service," Barbara Shore told *Pitt Magazine* in 1987. (document courtesy of Joan Shames)

Shore was also an early leader in the civil rights and anti-war movements. She was arrested during civil rights marches. Her name is inscribed on the Freedom Corner monument, which marks the line where demonstrators from the Hill District held back urban renewal efforts in the 1960s. She regularly wrote letters to local newspapers and appeared on local radio and television programs to speak out against the Vietnam War.

Among the many honors she received for her work, Shore once said she took particular pleasure in two: winning the Hannah G. Solomon Award from the NCJW in 1987 and being named a Distinguished Service Professor by the University of Pittsburgh upon her retirement in 1992. Tellingly, both honors celebrated her accomplishments in community service and her ability to utilize her profession to address societal needs.

[Editors' Note: Joan Shames is a sister of Dr. Barbara Shore.]

SOURCES:

Shore, Barbara K., oral history interviews, 1993, *Pittsburgh and Beyond: the Experience of the Jewish Community*, National Council of Jewish Women, Pittsburgh Section, Oral History Collection at the University of Pittsburgh (http://images.library.pitt.edu/cgi-bin/i/image/image-idx?view=entry;cc=ncjw;entryid=x-ais196440.426)

"Top Hat, White Tie, and Tales," *The Carnegie Tartan,* January 12, 1943, p. 6

"Barbara K. Shore," profile by NASW Social Work Pioneers [http://www.naswfoundation.org/pioneers/s/shore.html, accessed Nov. 29, 2015]

Shore, Barbara K., oral history interview, In Sisterhood Project (http://www.insisterhood.info/historical-library/activist-histories/leaders/barbara-shore/)

"Obituary: Barbara K. Shore / Pitt professor defended the most vulnerable," by Bill Schackner, *Pittsburgh Post-Gazette*, October 25, 2013

Authors

Prior to her retirement in the 1990s, **Jane Callomon Arkus** was senior vice president, creative director of the Pittsburgh office of Burson Marsteller, an international marketing communications agency. She is a graduate of Vassar College, where her studies in sociology and "Contemporary Press" spurred her to seek a career in communications and the art of persuasion. Over her six-decade career she has led campaigns for a wide range of clients—consumer, business-to-business and non-profit products and services. Working with the late Bernice Preisser, she steered strategic planning and programs for such leading Jewish institutions as the Jewish Commission on Aging, National Council of Jewish Women, Montefiore Hospital and Rodef Shalom Congregation. Through the years she has accrued many national and regional honors, has sat on many community boards and is currently deeply involved in board work for The Pittsburgh Cultural Trust. In 2002, then-Governor Tom Ridge named her a Distinguished Daughter of Pennsylvania.

Martha L. Berg has been the Archivist of Rodef Shalom Congregation in Pittsburgh since 2001. She has a Bachelor's degree in Religion from Smith College, a Master's in International Administration from the School for International Training and a Master's in Library and Information Science with Archives specialization from the University of Pittsburgh. She has worked as an Archivist for the Heinz History Center and the Pittsburgh Symphony Orchestra and is an archives consultant for families and non-profit organizations. She has published articles on Pittsburgh's Jewish history and on American Transcendentalism.

Carol Stein Bleier's paternal ancestors arrived in Pittsburgh from Eastern Europe in the early 1900's. Born and raised in New York, she received her Bachelor's degree in English literature from Syracuse University and a Master's degree from the School of Information Sciences at the University of Pittsburgh. A writer, researcher and public relations specialist, she worked in public relations for the Internal Revenue Service in Washington D.C. Her published works include numerous magazine and newspaper articles as well as four corporate histories. Among them are *The Ketchum Spirit*, the story of the international advertising agency Ketchum Communications Inc.; *L'Chaim: To Good Heath and Life, A History of Montefiore Hospital of Pittsburgh, Pennsylvania, 1898-1900*; and *Tradition in Transition: A History of the School of Information Science*. She is listed in the Marquis *Who's Who of American Women*.

Laura Cherner is currently a student at the University of Pittsburgh. She is a political science major and French minor and is working towards her Jewish Studies Certificate. Many of her studies have a focused on Jewish figures in politics and the American Jewish experience. Additionally, she spent a summer semester in France studying the French language and culture in the city of Nantes. She is originally from Squirrel Hill but now lives with her family in Mt. Lebanon. Laura hopes to pursue a future in law and continue her involvement with the Jewish community of Pittsburgh.

Frances Aaron Hess was born and raised in Pittsburgh. She was a governor of the Hebrew Union College-Jewish Institute of Religion, an honorary governor of the American Jewish Committee and an honorary vice-president of its New York Chapter, a trustee of Congregation Emanu-El of New York and served on numerous educational and cultural boards. Hess died during the production of this book and is greatly missed.

Born in Pittsburgh, **Susan Friedberg Kalson** is a graduate of Harvard College and the University of Pittsburgh School of Law. She is a lifelong member of Rodef Shalom Congregation, which she served as president from 2004-2006. Since its founding in 2006, she has been the Chief Executive Officer of the Squirrel Hill Health Center, a non-profit, federally funded community health center providing primary medical, behavioral health, and dental care to a diverse population, regardless of insurance status or ability to pay. She serves on numerous boards, including the Pennsylvania Association of Community Health Centers, of which she is currently the Vice Chair, and the Commission on Social Action of the Union for Reform Judaism, where she chairs the Israel and World Affairs Task Force. She lives in Squirrel Hill with her husband David, a lawyer whose Jewish Pittsburgh roots also trace back to the 1880's. They are the proud parents of three grown children.

Dr. Rachel Kranson is a professor of religious studies at the University of Pittsburgh, where she teaches courses in modern Jewish history, American religions and gender studies. Along with Hasia Diner and Shira Kohn, she is the co-editor of *A Jewish Feminine Mystique?: Jewish Women in Postwar America* (Rutgers University Press, 2010). Her current manuscript, under contract with the University of North Carolina Press, focuses on American Jewish upward mobility in the decades after World War II. Additionally, she is working on a project tracing the Jewish interventions in debates over reproductive rights.

Corinne Azen Krause taught history at Carnegie Mellon University and at the University of Pittsburgh. She received a B.A. from the University of Michigan, an M.A. from Carnegie Mellon University and a Ph.D. from the University of Pittsburgh. Her research is focused on Jewish communal history in Pittsburgh, particularly on Jewish women. Among her publications are *Grandmothers, Mothers, and Daughters*, an oral history study of three generations of Jewish Italian and Slavic women; and *Los Judios en México*, a Spanish translation of her dissertation on the history of Jews in Mexico.

Eileen Lane has deep roots in Pittsburgh and a long history of volunteer service in its Jewish and general community. A graduate of the Ellis School and Goucher College, she did her graduate work in the Religious Studies Department of the University of Pittsburgh. She has written articles on Soviet Jewish women, the status of women in Pittsburgh's Jewish community and Jewish immigration to Pittsburgh. She has a particular interest in women's health and education. She has served on many non-profit boards, chaired the boards of the Ellis School and the Family Health Council and was the first woman president of Rodef Shalom Congregation.

Eric Lidji is a writer and researcher. For many years, he has been a consultant for the Rauh Jewish Archives at the Heinz History Center, where he provided research for the website *A Tradition of Giving: A History of Jewish Philanthropy in Pittsburgh*, curated the website *Generation to Generation* and is currently writer and oral historian for the Small Towns Jewish History Project, an initiative to document Jewish life in small towns throughout Western Pennsylvania. He has also conducted research for the National Council of Jewish Women, Pittsburgh Section, and Rodef Shalom Congregation.

Lois G. Michaels began her professional life after graduating from Pennsylvania College for Women, now Chatham University. She taught history, worked in educational publishing and earned a graduate degree in public health that led her to found and lead the Health Education Center, which became a non-profit affiliate of Highmark Blue Cross Blue Shield. An enthusiastic Pittsburgher, she has served as president of Ladies Hospital Aid Society and a trustee of University of Pittsburgh Medical Center, Rodef Shalom Congregation and Western Pennsylvania School for Blind Children. She has awards from the National Council of Negro Women, the Jewish Healthcare Foundation and both her alma maters, among others. She is married to Dr. Milton Michaels, the mother of three and the grandmother of four. The sudden loss of vision has not deterred her from leading an active life into her 80's.

Until she was 18 years old, **Ruth Cooper Reidbord** lived in Leechburg, Pa., in Armstrong County, as one of very few Jewish girls in the community. She attended and was confirmed by the Southwestern District of Pennsylvania Jewish Religious Schools, attended Bucknell University and was graduated from the Margaret Morrison Carnegie College of the Carnegie Institute of Technology, now Carnegie Mellon University. She received a Masters in Urban and Regional Planning from the Graduate School of Public and International Affairs and was one of the first Jewish women in Pittsburgh to receive accreditation from the American Institute of Certified Planners. She served as Planning Director in Mt. Lebanon for over 24 years (the first woman to hold the position) and then began a consulting career in planning. She was a board member of Temple Emanuel and Temple Sinai and was president of the Tri-State Federation of Reform Temples of the Union of American Hebrew Congregations (now the Union for Reform Judaism). She has served on many committees in the Jewish community and continues to study with the IEngage program of the Hartman Institute of Israel. She has taught a class in urban planning at Osher/CMU for over 10 years and is a former board member of Osher.

Joan Shames is a native of Pittsburgh. She attended Allderdice High School and the University of Pittsburgh, where she earned a B.A. in English Literature and a M.S. in Audiology and Speech Pathology. She was president of the Falk School PTA and of the Allderdice High School PTA. She worked in Cincinnati and in St. Louis, and returned to Pittsburgh to work at the University of Pittsburgh. After retiring, Ms. Shames volunteered with the heart transplant program at Pitt, doing post-transplant interviews with heart transplant patients. She was also a volunteer at the National Council of Jewish Women-sponsored Children's Playroom in the courts in Pittsburgh.

Edie Shapira MD is a psychiatrist who has worked in private practice since 1991 and has been active in the community in a wide variety of roles. She received her Bachelor's Degree from Oberlin College, and her MD from the University of Pittsburgh School of Medicine. She completed her residency in Psychiatry at Western Pennsylvania Psychiatric Clinic. She is a Clinical Assistant Professor of Psychiatry at the University of Pittsburgh School of Medicine. She is the first woman Board Chair of The Pittsburgh Foundation and has served on many boards, including the Allegheny County Board of Health, the Pittsburgh Promise, Riverlife, the City-County Sports and Exhibition Authority, the Urban League of Greater Pittsburgh and the Western PA Conservancy.

The members of the Jewish Women's History Project Advisory Committee are Martha Berg, Carol Bleier, Rachel Colker, Marcia Frumerman, Andrea Glickman, Frances Aaron Hess, Rachel Kranson, Eileen Lane, Eric Lidji, Susan Melnick, Lois Michaels and Ruth Reidbord.

Index

Aaron, Marcus, 7

Aaron, Marcus Lester, 6-7

Aaron, Maxine Goldmark, 5-14

Adlow family, 63, 66

advertising, 139-145, 196

African Americans, 2, 69, 185

aliyah, 42-43

Allderdice High School, 7, 82, 176, 188, 200

Allegheny City, 114, 158

Allegheny County: Commissioner, 134; Court of Common Pleas, 8, 15, 17, 22-23, 134; Office of Children, Youth, and Families, 176, 191; tax office, 134

Alpern, Anne X., 15-26

Alter, Sadie, 158-159, 161

American Association of University Women, 69, 77-78

American Jewish Joint Distribution Committee, 40-41

American Jewish Outlook, 36

American Medical Association, 78, 120

anti-Semitism, 29, 97, 108, 116, 118. *See also* discrimination against Jews

Arkus, Jane C., 89-95, 139-145, 195

artists, 79-88, 89-95, 126

Associated Artists of Pittsburgh, 83, 85, 94

Austria-Hungary, 5, 158

baseball, 126, 137, 188

Baum, Charlotte, 3

Beard, Charles, 2

Beard, Mary Ritter, 2

Berg, Martha L., 57-62, 172, 195, 200

Beth Hamedrash Hagodol, 29

Biblical Botanical Garden (Rodef Shalom), 96, 98-104

birth control, 111-112, 150

Bleier, Carol Stein, 27-37, 96-105, 196, 200

blind people, 59-60, 147, 199

B'nai Israel Congregation, 31, 36, 176

Board of Education (Pittsburgh), 7-14, 164

Boston, 63-64, 66, 68, 93

Braddock, PA, 167

WA